# Calamity's Daughters
## Women Who Lead Despite Adversity

*An Anthology with*
*Stories of Resilience and Hope*

Kingdom Builders Publications LLC

Copyright © 2018 Calamity's Daughters – Women Who Lead Despite Adversity

Anthology Writers

Kingdom Builders Publications, LLC

All rights reserved. No part of this book may be reproduced or transmitted in any form or by any means without written permission from the author.

Printed in the USA

Second Edition

Soft Cover ISBN 978-0-692-15788-6

Library of Congress Control Number 2018936857

**Authored by**
Delores Brown
Juanita Frazier
Dr. Yvonne F. Keitt
Venis Livingston
Victoria Owens
Robinette Rankin

**Editors**
Kingdom Builders Publications
Dr. Lakisha Forrester
Louise Smith

**Photographer**
L H Photography

**Cover Design**
LoMar Designs

Bible Gateway. (n.d.) Versions/Amplified Bible. Retrieved from https://www.biblegateway.com/versions/Amplified-Bible-AMP/#booklist

Gregory, C. (2018). The five stages of grief: An examination of the Kübler-Ross Model. Retrieved from https://www.psycom.net/depression.central.grief.html

# DEDICATION

This book is dedicated to all the amazing women who find themselves in challenging and difficult paths in their journey called life. We are here to walk alongside you as you move forward with determination, with every brave step to a new bright dawn on your future of hope. There is indeed light and joy in the morning. *Dr. Yvonne F. Keitt*

I dedicate this book to God Almighty who helped me through this journey and all the women who have traveled the road of the loss of a loved one, particularly a loss due kidney diseases. I dedicated this book to my beloved parents, family, and sisters. I am so proud of all my blood-sisters for all the achievements in their lives. This is a testimony that God was with us and guided our steps in life. *Victoria Owens*

I dedicate my story to my mother, sisters, and children. To the women who feel they have no voice or identity in the mist of their darkness, I dedicate it to you as well. I hope these events of my life serve not as a cautionary tale, but as a testimony of God's mercy and grace. His grace will lead the hurt and bewildered, the raped and beaten, the lost and unloved to His loving arms. I dedicate this part of my life to my sisters of this world who might not see the beauty in the Darkness. No matter what you may go through in life, because you are a daughter of God, you are a queen. Although your crown may get dusty and sometimes dented, pick yourself up, polish that crown, and sit on your throne as the rightful queen of your destiny. I love you all. *Robinette Rankin*

I would like to thank those who followed me on my journey and supported my dream. I dedicate this book to all people who are going through a challenging and difficult situation. I want you to know God can and will strengthen you as you face your situations. You will have victory! This dedication is for those who stepped out in faith and hope to influence this work, the **Calamity's Daughters** project. *Venis Livingston*

I give the glory to my Lord and Savior Jesus Christ who has given me the wisdom and strength to write my story in hopes to reach out to women and let them know they can overcome in any situation. *Delores Brown*

This dedication is to the passion of a woman who refuse to take abuse anymore, some may have died for that freedom; I celebrate the love of a GOD who kept me through all my mess and messed up situations, to the memory of my birth and surrogate parents, to all my sons and daughters; given and chosen, and to my *was*-band and husband. I love you all. *Juanita Frazier*

## CONTENTS

|   | Dedication | iii |
|---|---|---|
|   | Acknowledgments | viii |
| 1 | Eleven – Eleven – Ninety | 10 |
| 2 | A Legacy of Serving Others in the Midst of Hard Times | 20 |
| 3 | Darkness Between the Memories | 30 |
| 4 | God Always Delivers | 61 |
| 5 | Ain' Nobody Told Me It Was Abuse | 71 |
| 6 | Beauty for Ashes: The Principles of Overcoming Grief and Loss | 97 |
|   | Resources | 108 |

**Calamity's Daughters – Women who Lead Despite Adversity** is a work of love presented by some incredible women telling some incredible stories. Here are a few women who symbolize bravery; they chose to move forward in their time regardless of their personal obstacles. You will hear the stories of loss, physical, verbal and sexual abuse, domestic violence, grief, suicidal thoughts, hopelessness, and harsh conditions in the workplace.

God is masterful in giving power and restoration to these women and letting others see the beauty that comes out of their ashes. This anthology is a testament on how the brokenness of these ladies is turned into a power of women that are very capable of leading their lives, their community, state, and nation.

My prayer is that the collection of stories in this anthology will give hope, encouragement, and resources to all who will walk this journey, and be a catalyst to other women on their journey to wholeness in their spirit, soul, and body.

May we continue to aspire, inspire, and impact every person in our circle of influence.

*Be Blessed,*
*Dr. Yvonne F. Keitt*

*And they overcame and conquered him because of the blood of the Lamb and because of the word of their testimony, for they did not love their life and renounce their faith even when faced with death.*
**Revelation 12:11 Amplified Bible (AMP)**

*If there ever comes a time when the women of the world come together purely and simply for the benefit of mankind, it will be a force such as the world has never known.*
**Matthew Arnold**

# ACKNOWLEDGMENTS

God is masterful and the author of every living thing, idea, and thereto, we are thankful for His faithfulness and grace as we present this body of work.

We are so thankful for every word of kindness, every prayer declared over this project to bring it to fruition. Without you, this anthology would not have been possible.

We acknowledge our Spiritual leaders and church families for your encouragement, support, and prayers. We love and thank you. This includes our family and friends. To all women who rise to lead despite their struggles, hardships, and the like. We walk along side you o your path to victorious living.

To Mrs. Louise Smith and Dr. Lakisha Forrester and the publishing staff at Kingdom Builders Publications, LLC; to Faith Hart, thank you for your dedication and hard work.

To all the brave women at Hannah House, the Director and Board of Advisors, no words can express our gratitude and love to each one of you. This project was birthed out of an event held for women to share their stories of resiliency, hope, and a belief that women who know or becoming to know their God will do great exploits in every sphere of influence.

# Story One

# ELEVEN – ELEVEN – NINETY

Where does one go when one's life turns upside down and inside out and straight to the bottom? The bottom is where there is no other place to go, but simultaneously finding it impossible to get back up. I found myself at the clutches of betwixt and between life and death, sorrow, and distress.

I was a woman who believed in making her own way. I worked three jobs, had two children to support as my mother took on some responsibility to help with her grands. I was still looking for that real opportunity, where the money worked for me instead of me working for it.

I never forgot that early Sunday morning in November 1990 when I got off work late. The events of that day led me to discover that, "No matter what happens to you in life, there is always another side to what God is doing. Sometimes you just hit a bump in the road." Those are the words that I speak so easily and freely now—the way I'd speak to a friend over a cup of coffee. In an honest, candid, and sometimes humorous manner, I confess that although I've had my share of bumps in the road, I am a living testimony that there is life after tragedy.

Born and raised in South Carolina, I traveled to New York for the summer when I was 13. While there, I met a young man who was also visiting from SC. He eventually became my husband. When I was 21, we got married and later had two children.

At first, the abuse was verbal. He would just say crazy things. As time progressed, mental and physical abuse came into the picture. A little push here and there quickly ballooned into full-blown aggression. Initially, this was a source of confusion for me. Why was this happening? Where was it all coming from? As the only child of my parents, I had never seen this behavior modeled in my home. My parents had a good relationship. I felt that my dad worshipped my mom, and my mom worshipped my dad. In fact, my dad, whom I was much closer to than my mother, had warned me that a man should never hit a woman. There were occasions where my aunts had been physically beaten, and my dad would drive up to New York or New Jersey to protect them. I even accompanied him on some of those weekend intervention trips. Now, I was the one being abused. I never told my father about the abuse, because I didn't want to upset him. He had suffered a stroke, so he wasn't able to be my protector.

For two to three years, I walked on eggshells in an effort not to upset him. At times, I wondered if I was the problem. I have to admit, I've got a mouth! I even began to wonder if perhaps my verbal assertiveness was perceived as a threat. Some family members even suggested that if I kept my mouth shut, it would be alright. But the old-fashioned mentality that it is OK for a man to hit a woman, just didn't sit well with me. I knew that it wasn't supposed to be like that. My body should not have to endure something like that.

In time, I enjoyed a budding friendship with another military wife who was also going through issues at home. Frequently, this friend shared that she was going to counseling, and she suggested that I go with her one day. That too, was a foreign concept. In my circle, you either went to church or talked with a family member if you had a problem. Seeking a counselor was not the norm. But, the physical abuse is what drove me to make that final step. I admit that he pulled my hair and dragged me on the floor. I knew that it was not OK for a man to do that to a woman, and I certainly didn't want my daughter and son thinking that it was OK either.

    I will never forget my first session at Sister Care. Each time the counselor asked me a question, he would wind a rubber band around his finger. The more questions he asked, the tighter and tighter the band got. He explained that once the rubber band popped, I could never put it back together again. To illustrate this, he used a lighter, a piece of tape, and a safety pin, one by one, to mend the rubber band. Nothing worked. Like that rubber band, if things continued along the same path, I would eventually break, and I would never be the same. I could have the house, the car, the clothes, and the kids—but I would never be the same. Yes, there was always medication, but that was no guarantee. Sometimes it worked, and sometimes it didn't. I had a choice to make. The counselor said he would leave that decision to me.

    Upon returning home, I was welcomed with accusations that I had been out with another man. Thinking quickly, I explained to my husband that I had to go to the USC campus to learn more about having a career. "What do you need a career for? I have enough money," he responded. Those were the types of behaviors that no one else saw. Knowing he had no desire to see me grow educationally, I knew that I couldn't improve myself. I felt like I couldn't grow. Again, this was in contrast to my parents, who had always told me that I could do and be anything that I wanted. In fact, my dad had always encouraged me to be better.

My grandma knew about the abuse. She used to tell me, "Let him hit you. Let it be. Don't start nothing." The abuse was concealed well to others. Everybody in my family thought I was crazy. In front of others, he was 'the man' but when we got home, he could detail everything that I did and said while we were out that he didn't like. Whenever we visited his family, he moved about freely, while I remained at the house. In instances where his sister wanted to take me out, he demanded to know where we were going and why. When I suggested to him that we get marriage counseling, he would protest and remind me that he is the reason for me having a Cadillac and clothes for the kids. He was also adamant that he didn't want people telling him what to do with his life.

"Watch the pattern," the counselor at Sister Care warned me. This advice proved to be life-changing for me. Armed with careful directions on what to look for, I began the process of observation, even color-coding things on my calendar. I only used the colors, red and blue. Red meant danger, while blue indicated good days. I discovered that he would go on cycles lasting three to four months. As he got closer and closer to the time, he would begin acting out, until he eventually exploded. I never could figure out what was going on in his life during those red color days to indicate why he was so explosive. Sometimes that man would come home late at night, waking me up, and wanting to fight. I recall that there was always something that I didn't do, according to him. Why didn't I lock the door? Or, why didn't I warm the food properly? It was always something.

After being married for ten years, my moment of escape was imminent. While he was overseas, I recruited two friends to help me move out and put my things in storage. Next, I filed for divorce. Moving back home near my mother, I began the process of rebuilding my life. Upon his return to the U.S., he moved to Washington where he began a relationship with another young lady.

I was able to meet her in person when they would come to get the children. One day they showed up to take the children to Washington without my knowledge. I panicked as I got to my mom's house and discovered my children were missing. No clothes were even packed for them. The only word that came to my mind was *kidnapping*, as I drove frantically on the interstate to his sister's home. I don't even know how I even got there safely. There was obvious road construction going on, and I found myself squeezing through traffic and signs to get to my babies. Once I arrived, in a state of rage, I began hitting him. There seemed to be glimpses of light appearing on his body at random places as if his body was a board used in target practice. Everywhere I saw a light, is where I hit him. Before I left his sister's home with my children, his lady said she liked my spirit. Two years later, his woman contacted me after they had a big fight on the base to tell me he had done the same thing to her.

In 1990, I was at the home of a co-worker who was doing an addition to her home. Prior to this day, she had threatened to leave her boyfriend on many occasions because he was abusing her. She used to hide clothes in her car, and then head to the homes of others after work. But, he seemed to always find her. On November 11, without warning, her boyfriend came into her home and began firing shots from his 38-revolver handgun. There were several family members and friends in the home at the time. She was shot point blank in the temple and killed. There was only one way out of the house. As I ran to escape and trying to get everyone out of the house, I was shot in the left side of the back of my head. I can honestly say that I don't remember a lot of what happened. Much of what I do know is what was told to me by the people in the home.

When I woke up, I was like a stroke patient. I recall being paralyzed on my right side. I couldn't walk. I suffered memory loss. I had double vision, and my speech was slurred. Despite losing a small portion of my brain, I fought to recover. It was obvious where I got shot in the head at, as it was an obvious entrance wound. However, there was no indication that the bullet ever escaped.

Churches in the east and west coast—New York, New Jersey, and California—prayed for my recovery and sent me cards and flowers. By the grace of God, and with minimal insurance, God allowed my medical care not to suffer. I was able to get the medical care and physical therapy needed without any out-of-pocket expenses. I spent two weeks in the hospital. There was a doctor who prayed for me and told me I would be able to see before I leave the hospital. I didn't even have to wear glasses as a result of the shooting. In fact, I just started wearing glasses in recent years because I am getting older. I spent three months at HealthSouth Rehabilitation Hospital.

There were many who prayed and many others were inspirational in helping me recover during physical therapy. I know that I am a miracle. The ambulance worker said that my ability to remain alert is what saved my life.

The shooter was sentenced to life for killing my friend, and got 20 years for shooting me. At present, from 28 years back, my friend's family and mine attend the parole hearings to ensure that he will not be released to hurt anyone else. The parole hearing happens every two years. As a ritual, we go to lunch and celebrate my dear friend's life. I think it's important to remember the families of the victims.

Although my left foot still has a drop, requiring me to wear a brace, I still proclaim that I am truly blessed. I believe it's so sad that some people do not know the Lord. Over all these years, I had nothing but wonderful people in my life. I know that God chose me to work with people. From time to time, I share my testimony in churches. I want to continue bringing awareness to domestic violence. I believe there should be programs to help women of all ages to learn to listen to their mind and body. I believe triggers occur which informs our senses that we are in danger. Staying and trying to fix it does not always work, sometimes it can end in death. In honor of her family and my own, I believe I have to use what happened to us to help others. I wholeheartedly believe that I represent two people—My spiritual angel and myself.

I've found that a lot of women need support as they too have dealt with some abusive issues. I am always astonished at just how being transparent and open will allow others to be comfortable in sharing their struggles. My friend tried to get a restraining order, but it was never followed up from her local authorities. I'm overwhelmed in sadness of the many women who tried to tell about their abuse, but they couldn't get the support and services they needed. My heart also aches for the ones who do not feel they are mentally strong enough to make a step towards protecting themselves and their families. I often think about the many who called and reported domestic violence while it was in progress, but the authorities either took too long to come to their homes or didn't come at all. That's why I continue to be a positive force in various communities, working with different organizations, in different cities having dialogue with women in the streets.

To this day, I have the assurance that there is always another side to what God is doing. Encouraged throughout the years by the 23rd Psalm, I emphasize that nobody could do this for me, but God. Today I can walk, drive, and have conversations with people. I know that those abilities are not because of what I know or the people I know—but, because of God! November 11, 1990 is a day I never will forget. It is also a day I look on and see how far God has brought me.

# MORE ABOUT THE AUTHOR

Venis Livingston, a low-country resident of South Carolina,  is an only child to her parents, Mr. & Mrs. Jamison. She is a mother of two and grandparent of seven, but she mentors and parents many over the east coast. Miss V, affectionately called by her peers and people whom she ministers to in the streets, is known throughout for being a community liaison.

Her hobbies include traveling, caring, serving, and worshipping her GOD.

Her heart's desire is to have a haven for people who are homeless, without clothes and other essentials.

She is best known as an advocate for battered and abused women and children. She is a part of the promotions department for the South Carolina Human Trafficking Resource Center, providing awareness.

For more information about Human Sex Trafficking or if you need help and services, please contact:

www.traffickingresourcecenter.org
Text: 233733 (BEFREE)
Telephone: 888-373-7888

lavernlivingston@gmail.com

# Story Two

# A LEGACY OF SERVING OTHERS
# IN THE MIDST OF HARD TIMES

Named by both of my grandmothers, my name is Martha Ann Queen Victoria. Everyone called me Victoria, but as the eldest daughter of my father, he called me *Centerpiece*. I often say that we get strength from God to do what we can for others, because God walks with us. My unwavering assurance of God's presence has served as an anchor throughout life's challenges, and has given me the drive and the passion to help others in need. I have devoted many years to ensuring that people get the healthcare they need. Much of my passion came center stage as I volunteered as an advocate for better healthcare within the 1199SEIU United Healthcare Workers East, a healthcare union with over 500,000 members.

My concern for others started me on a new journey. Describing myself as politically active, in 2004, the needs that I saw in my community compelled me to campaign for John Kerry in Florida. I wanted a better community in general—a good education for our young people, prescriptions for seniors, and affordable housing for everyone. The property taxes and unemployment were extremely high in the community. It was a campaign that we lost, but I was not deterred.

In 2005, while Hillary Clinton was a senator in New York, they needed a retiree to represent them at a Democratic forum on Social Security reform. This forum was in response to

President George W. Bush's plans to privatize Social Security. I served as a representative at this forum which drew over 800 people to Pace University in Manhattan, and made the NY Times front page. In 2008, I continued my political service as I traveled to Milwaukee, WI, to campaign for the future 44th president, Barack Obama. I also served in South Bend, IN as a proponent for Obamacare.

Throughout my travels, I was keenly aware of God's presence with me. Traveling to other states and campaigning for various candidates not only allowed me to serve my community, but it also helped me to heal and have a renewed sense of purpose. While I was in Florida campaigning, a hurricane came through the area. Although my hotel was hurricane safe, my dad told me to take my Bible and a blanket, and go into the closet. When I woke up the following day and looked out of the window, I saw palm trees, but everything else looked like it had been run over by a tractor-trailer. That was yet another moment where I knew it was just God and me.

God has always been there for me. That was no different when I married Wilson Owens in September 1987. Wilson was born in Tuskegee, Alabama. He had a disease as a child, which damaged one of his kidneys. My understanding is that the kidney disease started when he was a child and probably triggered when he had chicken pox or measles at seven years old. Wilson was taken to the doctor but health care was not readily accessible for people of color in the south at that time in history. This didn't affect him much while he was growing up, but in 1990, things began to change. After a series of events, the doctors determined that he would need a kidney transplant. It saddened me that I was unable to donate a kidney for my husband since I was a diabetic and may need the kidney later in life. He applied for a transplant and was put on a waiting list.

While receiving care at St. Joseph's Hospital in Yonkers, Wilson and I made plans, upon his discharge, to visit my father in South Carolina. As an EKG technician, I was knowledgeable about the treatments Wilson would need while we were traveling. Therefore, I was careful to make the necessary arrangements with each treatment center. Those plans were coming along nicely. One day, after visiting Wilson at the hospital, I went home to rest. At 3 a.m., the ring of the telephone jolted me from my sleep. The voice on the other end said words that I was neither expecting nor prepared for. "Mrs. Owens, we have sad news. Mr. Owens passed away." My dear husband was 52 years old, and had waited almost seven years for a kidney that he never got.

I remember being numb and all alone in the house. Our sons were all grown up and lived in different places. Robert was in Syracuse, Gerald was in Albany, and Kenny was in Iraq. Because it was so early in the morning, the only thing I could think of at the time was to call my father.

When I called my dad, he told me not to worry, and that they will be there as soon as possible. As I hung up the telephone, I was met with a profound feeling of loneliness. I was in shock at how quickly everything had transpired. I felt completely alone. Later, I called Gerald and Robert. I had to go through military procedure to inform Kenny.

I felt even more devastated to get the news that they received a kidney from a donor two weeks after the passing of my husband. My thoughts were, "He is dead now and why did he have to wait seven long years?" I thought back to how I kept calling his doctor to get the status on the kidney and was told they were still waiting for a donor. Wilson was the type of person that loved helping people so I decided to donate his eyes to the Eye Bank. Signing up Wilson to be an organ donor made me feel this act was an opportunity to give back to others.

I admit every time I thought about it; it made me cry. The period of grieving and mourning took time. It was difficult to go through the grieving process. There were times when I thought about Wilson and it brought tears to my eyes. I remember a particular incident on the bus when I started crying and people around offered me support. They checked on me to see if I was ok. I would then try to convince them that the reason for my tears was that my allergies were acting up. Friends would say, "Vickie, we are with you. We know this is a hard time for you."

There would be times I would see my friends with their husbands and get very sad that Wilson was not with us any longer. There was definitely a lot of denial going on. "Maybe this is not happening," I would tell myself. Then there was the juxtaposition of my emotions. One part of me knew it was true, but the other part of me didn't want to believe it. My father had to encourage me to get rid of Wilson's clothes, because I needed to come to grips with the fact that he was not coming back. It took some time before I was able to donate his clothes because I wanted to protect his belongings. Eventually, I gave his favorite jacket to my father. Wilson loved music. He and our cat, Frisky, would listen to music together. His favorite band was the Commodores because he played the drums with them in Alabama before the group became famous. I did keep some of his music for myself.

Although this was a rather difficult time, I was grateful to have family that could travel to my side. I made many visits to the gravesite on Wilson's birthday. Wilson's birthday was on February 2nd, Groundhog's day. I would also go on holidays and every week for a couple of years. He was my best friend and husband; and the gravesite was a beautiful place with a lake. I thought a lot during this time about the other women who didn't have anyone they could turn to when tragedy strikes.

I still describe our marriage as being a wonderful union of matrimony and friendship. I have fond memories of Wilson. Wilson was smart and good looking. When we walked down the street, women couldn't help but to look and stare at him. He was the senior store keeper in his department. Therefore, he was responsible for ordering all the supplies at the hospital. He was even recognized with an award from Harlem Hospital Center for twenty-five years of dedicated services.

He was not only my husband, but he was also my friend. That made such a difference. We always did things together. If we had a disagreement, we made up before we went to bed. Neighbors described us as being two peas in a pod, and there was an unspoken rule: no one could say anything bad to Victoria about Wilson, and vice versa. Oftentimes, the nature of in-law relationships can be volatile. But, this was not an obstacle for us as a pair. He had a good family. He had a wonderful mother and sisters. My father loved him like a son, and my sisters loved him like a brother. Very much a people person, Wilson loved others, and others loved him.

The relationship with my mom was very good. The children in our home was not allowed to cook. Our mother did all the cooking. We were responsible for cleaning, ironing, and washing clothes. I remember all the girls in our house had many dresses. Thus, we wore dresses all the time. When our mother died, our grandmother did the cooking for us. I didn't learn how to really cook until I was in my 20's. I went to Boston at 17 years old, because I really wanted to leave South Carolina. Every young person was leaving our hometown, which we thought was a boring place.

When my mother died at age 38 from a heart attack, I was 21 years old and I came home from Boston to live with my dad for six months to help out. My mother was diagnosed with juvenile diabetes as a child. I believe this condition contributed to heart disease. My friend, Vivian Wright, who I met in Boston, said she wanted to help support us with the tragedy of our mother's death. She stayed in the family home for six months to help us. In our community, many family and friends were there to offer support and guidance. Our community was like a village—everyone caring and helping each other.

I lived with my dad until he remarried. Later in life, he was diagnosed with a form of cancer that wasn't considered to be aggressive. In fact, he stayed in remission for seven years before the cancer returned. He cared deeply for his wife, Ruby, and didn't want to leave her. He always was there to provide support and guidance to her and other people in general. My father, a strong and determined personality, requested to die at home and not in the hospital. In fact, he was adamant about it. He wanted to make sure Ruby was taken care of after his death.

I promised my father that we would do whatever was necessary to ensure Ruby was taken care of if something happened to him.

The family stuck together and made arrangements during this difficult time. Maryann, my sister, gave up her apartment to help take care of him, and I would travel back and forth from NY to visit. I believe God was telling me something was going to happen, because I heard a lot of noise on the balcony of my apartment and I saw a huge angel. Three months later, my father called and said the cancer had returned.

I remember that last phone call I had with my dad. I recall that it took all of my strength as I cried and pleaded with my father to give up and go home to God. After hanging up the phone, my dear father closed his eyes for the last time. Shortly after his passing, my baby sister called me about the news. This was devastating, shocking news. It was just heartbreaking—too much to take in. I didn't want to hear it. My father just left the earth. I tell you death is something you never get used to.

My sisters and I always had a close relationship with our dad. Since our mother died at such a young age, our father was everything and was so precious to each one of us. He loved people and enjoyed mentoring young people. His standards for his daughters were high. "Always present yourself as a lady at all times," is what he would tell us. He even taught me how to dance. We used to talk for hours on the telephone, sometimes until 2 a.m. He was the backbone of the family and had an amazing sense of humor.

Losing my parents and my husband was difficult. God is the one who gives me the strength. The scriptures, particularly Psalm 91, provided the bedrock of support for me in the coming days and years.

When I was 62 years old, I had a conversation with my father about me retiring. My father told me that I should take into consideration, prior to making a decision, that some people were not fortune enough to live until they were 65 to retire. He said it would be nice to retire when your health is good, since he has seen people who haven't made it to 65. After our discussion, I made the final decision to retire at the same age he retired—age 62.

I always had a heart-driven desire to advocate for seniors to ensure their needs were addressed. To this day, I continue to look around and see the needs in my community to do what I can for others, and I continue to challenge others to do so as well. As I see the population of seniors growing around me, I envision more senior activity centers being built, volunteer programs being developed, certificate programs being offered, and anything else that would make their lives easier.

## Psalm 91 KJV

1 He that dwelleth in the secret place of the most High shall abide under the shadow of the Almighty.
2 I will say of the LORD, He is my refuge and my fortress: my God; in him will I trust.
3 Surely he shall deliver thee from the snare of the fowler, and from the noisome pestilence.
4 He shall cover thee with his feathers, and under his wings shalt thou trust: his truth shall be thy shield and buckler.
5 Thou shalt not be afraid for the terror by night; nor for the arrow that flieth by day;
6 Nor for the pestilence that walketh in darkness; nor for the destruction that wasteth at noonday.
7 A thousand shall fall at thy side, and ten thousand at thy right hand; but it shall not come nigh thee.
8 Only with thine eyes shalt thou behold and see the reward of the wicked.
9 Because thou hast made the LORD, which is my refuge, even the most High, thy habitation;
10 There shall no evil befall thee, neither shall any plague come nigh thy dwelling.
11 For he shall give his angels charge over thee, to keep thee in all thy ways.
12 They shall bear thee up in their hands, lest thou dash thy foot against a stone.
13 Thou shalt tread upon the lion and adder: the young lion and the dragon shalt thou trample under feet.
14 Because he hath set his love upon me, therefore will I deliver him: I will set him on high, because he hath known my name.
15 He shall call upon me, and I will answer him: I will be with him in trouble; I will deliver him, and honour him.
16 With long life will I satisfy him, and shew him my salvation.

# MORE ABOUT THE AUTHOR

Victoria Owens is a passionate advocate, politician, and speaker. She has always been drawn to helping others and is described by her sisters as having a heart of gold. She has spent over three decades in the health field as an EKG Technician. Victoria's passion came center stage as she worked as an advocate for better healthcare within a healthcare union. She has been actively supporting and advocating for issues facing American families and seniors for many years. Councilman Andy King saw the passion of Owens and asked her to come aboard, of which she is thankful for the opportunity. She presently serves as a Council Aide with the 12th District Bronx, New York. Victoria is a widow and the mother of three grown sons – Gerald, Robert, and Kenny.

# Story Three

# DARKNESS BETWEEN THE MEMORIES

T hey say your past helps shape who you are today, and who you will be tomorrow. They say your past doesn't have to define you—that what doesn't kill you makes you stronger. Well, I can honestly say for me, all these sayings are true. My memories have shown me my past, and they have stripped me down to my rawest, most vulnerable place. My memories have revealed why I make certain decisions, and they have shaped who I've become and who I'm trying to be. With certainty, these memories could have shattered my mind into irreparable pieces. But I'm here, mended and stronger.

My earliest memory was as a toddler, not much older than three. My mother would drop me off at the top of my grandmother's long driveway. Wearing only a diaper, shirt, and shoes, I remembered being happy. Back then, life was blissful. Being the eldest grandchild, I felt loved, adored even. Excitement filled the air when my uncle would take us out on the sea in his speedboat. Then there were the times my mom took us to work on the party boat and I watched her perform her fire dance. I remember thinking, "I want to do that when I grow up." On the day my mom married my youngest sister's father, I even remember stealing the little edible pearls off the wedding cake. I also remember family photo day when I cried and cried because the flash made my eyes hurt and gave me a headache. Later, my eyes were tested for glasses. There were also memories that were a little sad, like for a very long time I didn't know when my birthday was. It was because for years it wasn't celebrated, I'm not sure why, but it felt normal. Yeah, I had great memories as a toddler—then Dark Memories.

It was a night I'd never forget; a memory no five-year-old should have. Although I do not recall the events leading up to my first Dark Memory, I remember my mom screaming while my stepfather beat her in the head with a meat tenderizer. I don't remember when he slit her throat with the knife, but I remember my grandmother rushing into the kitchen, yelling something while holding my mom's throat, then nothing. I don't remember the plane ride from my home island, Grand Cayman, to Jamaica. I don't remember who took us, and I don't even remember how we got to the woman we would call Grandma. I remember the fear of that night…the first time I felt lost…the first time my heart broke.

Living in Jamaica was good at first. We lived in a parish called May Pen and I attended a school called May Pen Primary School. I hated the school. It operated in shifts: morning shift, second shift, and third shift. Walking to school took forever as we climbed up and down large hills, and meandered through gullies in the sweltering heat. My sister, the middle child, and I were on the morning shift. We grew up without our youngest sister. My sister and I would experience horrible things together, grow to resent each other, and I would even grow to hate her. But for now, at five years old, I would walk with her to school, take care of her, and we would entertain each other.

There were many fond memories. I remember making doll clothes out of old plastic bags, and making clay with the red dirt that surrounded the house. We even used cow patties—dried cow poop—as frisbees, and we loved it. We would walk to Kingston, the capital city, and go to the market. Those days were amazing. We ate delicious local treats, such as bag ice, bag juice, sugar cane, and 'bun and cheese'. Occasionally, we would get a new church dress or a new doll. Living with two older boy cousins made life interesting, as they taught us how to catch lizards and provoke them with sticks to hear them squeal.

I also remember our uncle telling us to put on our special t-shirts. That meant two things: first, we got to play, and then, we got to eat chicken. Living in Jamaica in those days, we didn't go to the store to buy chicken; but rather, we raised our own. So, on the days we ate chicken, Uncle V had to kill one. To do this, he hung the chicken by the neck from a tree, then he chopped the head off. After that, we played a game to see who could catch the body before it stopped moving. When a chicken loses its head, the body runs wild for a few minutes afterwards, splashing blood everywhere; hence the special shirts. I remember when my mom's brother, Uncle Barry, came and built my first shower outside. That was so exciting. The water was always cold, but at least we didn't have to catch our water and wash up in a basin. Uncle Barry loved me, and I knew I was his favorite. Yeah, good memories. But as I tell my story, you will see a pattern. There will be good—even great memories—then Dark Memories.

One night, I remember getting up to use the bathroom, as I'd done many times before. This night, however, was different. Uncle V, tall and black with waist-long dreads, caught me as I came out of the bathroom. He led me to the kitchen, and he placed me on a piece of cardboard. He kissed me all over my face, told me how sweet I was, and warned me not to make any noise. As he raped me, I remember the searing pain I felt, and how foreign it was for him to be inside me. Aside from an occasional hiss of pain, I didn't cry. Afterwards, he told me to wash up and go to bed. I fell straight to sleep as if nothing had happened. The following day, I bled on my panties, but since I was responsible for handwashing my own clothes, no one else knew. This marked the start of what my life would be like going forward, and it would get worse.

Those two boy cousins that I spoke about earlier became molesters to both my sister and me. They never penetrated me, but they would remove my panties and rub themselves against me. I remember it feeling good. One day Uncle V caught us, which resulted in a severe beating from both him and my grandma. The beating, which seemed to last forever, left me black and blue with cuts where the belt welted me. A few nights later, after being raped again, Uncle V told me that if I ever let anyone else touch me, he would stop loving me, and he would kill me. I told him that I was sorry, and I remember loving the way he looked while he was inside me, because I was making him feel good. Sometimes I wouldn't want to be with Uncle V, and didn't want to deal with the pain, so I would purposely wet the bed. I did this knowing my grandma would beat the crap out of me, and make me hand-wash the sheets. Sometimes, one pain was more bearable than the other was.

This was life for a while. The beatings, administered with hoses or extension cords, were brutal, and left me bruised and bleeding. Sometimes, the beatings were directed at my head. The rapes now happened often enough to feel wrong, and I began to notice that my sister got better treatment than I did.

As I got older, I discovered that this was because she had light skin, while mine was very dark.

Things got scary when Uncle D, the father of my boy cousins, came to visit. He was tall, good looking, had pretty hair, dressed nicely, and smelt good too. He looked nothing like his brother. At first, he was fun. He took us to the market and bought us many things. He would play with us and chase us around. It felt like a breath of fresh air, especially since Uncle V left while he was there. Later, I learned that the brothers hated each other because their mother treated one better than the other because of their skin color. Soon, there were Dark Memories.

On this particular Saturday, our Sabbath, my grandma went somewhere after church and we were all supposed to go take a nap. I wasn't sleepy, so I went to the kitchen where Uncle D was. He put me on his lap and started tickling me, and then he stuck his finger in my panties and started rubbing me. Instantly I felt guilty, knowing if Uncle V found out, he would beat me, and maybe worse, stop loving me. My Uncle D told me to go to bed and take a nap. He said that if I wanted him to take me to the market again, I wouldn't say anything. Truthfully, I didn't care if he ever took me to the market again. I was petrified of what would happen if Uncle V found out. That same night Uncle D came for me, and picked me up out of my bed. He didn't lead me to the kitchen, but rather to my grandma's room, and placed me on the bed. He did things I'd never experienced before. He took off all my clothes, caressed me, and stuck his tongue in my mouth. It felt wrong. I remember thinking that he didn't love me like Uncle V did. Uncle V told me nice things and said he would take care of me. All I could think was, "I'm going to die. Uncle V is going to kill me." Uncle D was cold. When he finished, he told me to get dressed and go to sleep.

I remember not going to sleep for the rest of Uncle D's visit. My mom visited us, and I remember her and Uncle V doing things in the bed next to us while we were supposed to be sleeping. I thought, "Oh, so mommy does it too?" Later I found out that the men I called my uncles, the boys I called my cousins, and the woman I called my grandma weren't kin to me at all. My grandma was actually a family friend who took my sister and me in while our mother recuperated from her injuries and later, a mental breakdown. Later, I learned that these same men, Uncle D and Uncle V, raped my mother during her childhood when this same woman was asked to take care of her. This added another layer to the hate I would have towards my mother.

When I was seven, my mother came for my sister and me. I was so happy because it seemed that my problems were over. I remember sitting on the bed in my new bedroom and telling my mother about what my uncles did. She said, "Don't worry about that now—you'll never see them again." I was confused. Was that all she was going to say? I desperately needed to understand more. Was this something all little girls went through? Was it normal? I felt confused in my own skin, and I wanted answers. Why did it feel good sometimes? But then, why did it seem wrong? But it couldn't be wrong because adults do it, and adults are always right. What was this act called anyway? Was I supposed to continue doing it? I couldn't simply turn off a switch and stop thinking about it.

Our new residence was a three-bedroom home located

behind Georgetown Hospital. I lived with my sisters, my mom, and my stepdad. My new best friend lived just up the street, and things were going well. Dark Memories soon took center stage. My stepfather seemed to dislike me greatly. Although he would dote on my sisters and buy them things, he never did that for me. He also enjoyed accusing me of doing things that I didn't do, like going into the refrigerator after bedtime. Once I stole $10 from my mom, and of course, I got caught. On the next Christmas, my stepfather bought football team cups for all of us. My youngest sister got the 49ers, his favorite team, and my other sister got the Dolphins. He bought me a Steelers cup, explaining through laughter, that I was a thief and sucked just as badly as they did. I ran into my room and cried. Christmas, birthdays, and other festivities were like that for me. Either my stocking had less than my sisters' stockings, or he alienated me from everything we did. At a later time, my mom separated from him due to domestic abuse. Then, he kidnapped my youngest sister, and I wouldn't see her for 12 years after that.

My life continued in such a way that there were only glimpses of good memories. We moved from house to house, each one seeming to look better than the last. With each move came new friends, and a new beginning, but the cycle continued. My mom had a problem—she couldn't be alone, and the men she chose to be with were all evil. I would either witness beatings or be molested by these men. By now, I thought being molested was the norm, so that didn't bother me as much as the blood, the screams, and the late nights of running from one boyfriend's home to another.

At this point, I had anger problems brewing beneath the surface. Because I was older, certain things became apparent to me—not because anyone told me, but because these things didn't feel right. I came to the realization that being molested wasn't right. I realized this when my mom's boyfriend, R, made me conduct oral sex. Even though I hated it, he liked it, and made me perform it often. This fueled an anger in me that would grow into pure hatred. Why was I always being told to do these things? I couldn't understand. I felt that everyone was looking at me, knew what I was doing, and hated me for it. If someone hated me, I would hate him or her back, and I'd do one more thing. I would fight them. I would try to hurt a person for making me feel this way.

At school, I fought all the time. A girl had the nerve to call me a name, and I let her have it. It felt so good to burst her lip, watch it bleed, and listen as she cried. The kids watching seemed to applaud me for doing it, and it made me feel powerful. That was a new emotion for me. We were very poor, so sometimes my school uniform was dirty, and as a child, I had a bad body odor. My eyes were pretty big, and I had a huge gap between my two front teeth. In short, I was a bully's dream. However, they soon found out that they teased me at their own risk. My anger was so fierce when fighting, that I wouldn't let up until I couldn't move physically. I hurt people badly and didn't feel bad or guilty afterwards. I would fight with knives and rocks—anything to cause optimum damage. After all that, I would head right back home and have to be subjected to these men who would use me anyway they saw fit. Hopelessness, disgust, loneliness, ugliness, and hatred became the make-up of my soul. I wanted to die. Then, more Dark Memories.

I was 11 years old when the last of my mother's boyfriends I would ever have to live with came into my life. T was my worst everything. One evening, my mom and her friends were watching the news in the living room of our West Bay home. That picture was vivid to me because they were all angry that a man who was suspected of killing a boy was being released from jail. They were convinced that he was getting away with murder. It seemed like the next day when I met T for the first time, coming downstairs in his boxers, I didn't pay him much attention. At this time, it had been a while since I was touched. I had great friends, and my mom gave me a lot of freedom. The first time T came at me, he did it jokingly, grabbing my breast and then apologizing. At 11, I was very developed, and didn't look my age. I later found out that once a child has been penetrated vaginally, the body speeds up the maturing process, getting the body prepared to be able to carry a child and give birth.

There was something about T that I just didn't like. Perhaps, it was because we got attention from mom when she didn't have a boyfriend. But in actuality, he was just evil. The first time T molested me, I didn't even resist. His finger didn't hurt badly, so I felt I could deal with it. I thought about the school week, and the uniforms I needed to wash. That time was the best of the worst, because every time after that was literally hell. T would brutally rape me, squeezing my breasts hard and pinning my hands behind my back with such force that I thought my back would break. He grabbed me by the throat, while simultaneously penetrating and threatening me. I'm not sure why he felt the need to do that. I learned early on that things would finish faster if I acted like I enjoyed it. I didn't cry, scream, or fight. I would just be. But T was rough with me, and I knew he liked it that way. Then I became sick of it.

We shared a broken-down house with some other people. The toilet never worked and was always filled with people's waste. My mom, my sister, T, and I all shared the same bedroom. One particular day, my mom left to go outside, and T started in on me. He wanted to give me a massage and I tried to knock his hands away. He persisted and started rubbing my behind. I got angry and slapped his hands. With brute force, he kicked me into a wall, and for the first time in my life, I screamed out because the pain to my head was so severe. Mom rushed in to see my face covered in blood and as I was screaming to tell her what happened, she threw her coffee on him. I never would forget how I felt in that moment. It seemed like the pain went away because my mom was going to do something. She was going to save me. They argued while I cleaned myself up and then I heard them having sex. My heart was broken. I was left with a golf-ball-sized knot on my head with a split dead center. Hatred for my mother grew inside of me, and I would feel that hate for many years to come.

My final straw with T was when we had to move into a four-wall shack. This shack had no electricity, no running water, no toilet, nothing. Our electricity came from running an extension cord from a neighbor's house. We had to walk to get clean water, and we used the bushes outside as a bathroom. A bedsheet served as a divider to separate my mom and T's side of the room from ours. That last night, T reached under the sheet, with my mom sleeping right next to him, and squeezed my breast so hard that it woke me up. He took me outside and raped me with my face in the ground. When he was finished, I threatened to tell my mom. He said, "If you tell her, I'll kill her, and I'll get away with it like I did when I killed that boy." I didn't care. I wanted him to kill us because I didn't want to live this way anymore. I made up my mind that I would tell.

When T went fishing for dinner the next day, I thought that was the right time. I took my mom aside and started to tell her everything. I told her that T was messing with me and that he wouldn't stop. She said she would get him and bring him back, so he could answer to these accusations. My sister was there, and she shared with me that T was messing with her as well. I remember being so excited as I asked my sister to tell Mommy. Finally, Mommy would believe me. I kept saying, "You are her favorite. She will believe you." She assured me that she would tell. When T and my mom returned, my words fired off like a machine gun, as I revealed everything he had been doing. T accused me of lying and said I was just angry because he didn't like me. Turning to my sister, I demanded that she tell her story, but she did not. That moment was the beginning of a lifelong resentment toward my sister. I know now that she was a scared little girl and didn't know what to do. But at that time, I just saw betrayal. My mom went outside with T and they spoke for a long time. When she returned, she told us to get in the car. She drove us to the home of T's cousin, and in the parking lot, she gave me an ultimatum. I could either live with T and stop the lying, or I could move in with my best friend. I chose my best friend, and I also chose to hate my mom like never before. My best friend and I were a year apart, she was 12 and I was 11 when I chose her over living with T. I met my best friend J the year I moved back from Jamaica, she and her family lived up the street from us.

I was 7 or 8 when I met J for the first time. We met at the three bedroom house behind the hospital, where I first told my mom about what uncle V and D was doing to me in Jamaica.

J and I became quick friends, her mother was a homemaker who loved her, loved her family, and loved me. Her dad was a fisherman. He even did competition fishing, catching swordfish. J also had a big brother. I remember the huge crush I had on him. He taught me how to back flip off the pier into the ocean. I remember one summer I made up a fake adoption form for both J's mom and my mom to sign. I would be adopted for two weeks, I made it seem as if it was all in fun, but it was my way of getting away from my stepfather.

Once again Dark Memories: A year a so later, what no one knew, including my mom, was that my best friend's dad, a man I trusted and loved, a man who treated me so kindly and included me in so many family functions, betrayed me. I remember how once again my world got clouded in darkness. One day, Mr. D, his daughter, and I were wrestling. We were having so much fun until he wrestled me on the bed while J ran off to hide. He grabbed my breast and bit it. I was so shocked, so much so that I ran outside and hid in the bushes next to the front door. J was in charge of watering the plants. When she sprayed me with the hose, I remember jumping up because the water was so cold. I was so embarrassed because J was laughing at me and because of the event that just happened. I tried to scramble a lie to tell her why I was hiding in the bushes. I didn't want her to know the hurt and shame I was feeling.

Here I am at 12 years old and living with J again. But only for a few weeks, I called my 18-year-old boyfriend and told him I was moving in. This was the first time I started having sex because I wanted to. He didn't know at the time, I was twelve. I lied to him, telling him that I was fifteen, and that he was taking my virginity. In a way, I truly believed that. Not long afterwards, my mom found out and I was forced to move to America to live with my biological grandmother.

When I moved to the states at thirteen, neither I nor anyone else knew that I was pregnant. My grandmother knew I was pregnant, her being a nurse and all, and because I was throwing up all over the place. I felt like I was going to die. During this time, I used to sleep on the bathroom rug next to the toilet and sometimes I would even fall asleep while hugging the toilet. I thought I was sick because I was in the U.S. and I missed my boyfriend.

My mom would call my sister and me. Even though I didn't want to speak with her, I did so because she would sneak my boyfriend on the phone. I think my mom did this to get in good graces with me. I also think that she could relate to me being in love at that age, it was as if she knew what it was like. My grandmother found out my boyfriend and I were still speaking by picking up the other line. That was the final time I would ever speak with him again or hear him telling me he loved me. I didn't even have a chance to say it back out loud, in fear of being heard. That was also the last time I would hear him telling me to keep his baby and that he will be coming for us. I was so happy because I knew it to be true. I remember feeling so alone, because I also knew it to be false. I later found out that one of the reasons I was shipped off was due to a condition my mom worked out. To keep my boyfriend out of jail for statutory rape, she promised that I would be sent off the Island and we wouldn't ever be in any contact.

My grandmother took me to a facility where I sat in the waiting room and looked at pictures of families and babies in different stages of a pregnancy. Being in this office was cold and dreary. There were pictures of women's reproductive parts on posters. There was one poster where you could see where the baby was inside of a pregnant woman. I remember feeling so embarrassed looking at those posters, so much so I would take quick little glances and drop my head. I remember hiding a smile because I was growing my love's baby inside me. I wanted to know what I was looking at, but I was so scared to ask my grandmother. I felt embarrassed because there were condoms and birth control posters plastered everywhere.

Twice before, my grandmother took me to a clinic. The first time was to verify I was pregnant, and the next time was to find out how far along I was. This time we went to a new place. I thought this was a new doctor's office. After placing me in a room, the doctor spoke with my grandmother. Because I was used to being spoken about and not spoken to, I naturally tuned them out and started daydreaming. My thoughts were interrupted when the doctor said, "So do you understand?" Not wanting my grandmother to be angry with me for not paying attention, I said yes. They took me to a room, made me remove my clothes, and put on a paper-like gown. Three nurses entered. The doctor told me not to be afraid, and that I would hear a loud machine and feel a pinch. When I saw the huge needle, I started to freak out. The doctor then told me that I would feel pressure, but that I should try not to move too much.

As I felt the pain, I cried and hugged the nurse who was holding me down tighter than I'd ever hugged my own mother. The corners of my eyes went black, and then I remember waking up with a woman on my right and a woman on my left.

I sobbed because I knew that something had changed. Shortly after, the doctor came to me explaining that I was no longer pregnant, and that I would bleed heavily and have clotting for a few days. I cried when I saw the clots because I thought they were pieces of my baby.

After the abortion, I tried every and anything to get back home. My grandmother was a night nurse. She would get home super late, sometimes early in the next day. I knew her schedule, so I planned a little party. I invited my neighborhood friends to come over and we broke out the blender and my grandmother's nicest Champaign glasses and made drinks. I had boys over, lights dimmed low, and music blasting. When she walked in, she saw a bunch of kids in her house, using her things, and messing up her house. You see, older Islanders are very proud and private people. They don't like people in their things; and they definitely don't like unruly children. She ran everyone off and cussed me out. When she asked me why, I told her the truth. "I did this, so you can send me back home." Instead, she raised her hand as far back as she could and slapped me across my face. It hurt, hurt for days. I remember that the sting of failing once again to get sent back to my Island was much worse. I remember giving in and saying to myself, I'm stuck now. I remember thinking maybe I should just try to live here, away from my love, with people who really don't like me. I remember feeling a familiar feeling like I was gonna hurt someone. I went to school the next week and got in a fight. I repeatedly slammed a girl's face in the gym room locker. I knew someone was going to pick on me, either because of my eyes, teeth, or accent. I just needed someone to say something, anything, and she happened to be the unlucky one.

My life didn't get easier in America; it was just different. I was still very angry, but with new things to fight about. Favoritism was still a big part of my home, continuously tearing down my self-esteem. Even though I was never molested again, I still remember the last time a man raped me. This time was different. A man, whom I did not know, hit me on my head, and raped me when I was fifteen. Sex changed for me that day. I decided to give myself to any guy who looked like he might want me. By giving myself away, I was in control. I would be the only one with control over my body. I remember saying, "It's my choice, not theirs."

At the age of sixteen, I had my first child. My grandmother gave me the choice whether to have an abortion or to have the baby. When I was given the choice, I thought, "It's my body, my baby, and I'm keeping him." And still there were Dark Memories.

I graduated at 18, and I gave birth to my daughter one month later. There were so many emotions. Although I was excited for a girl, I was depressed and nervous, but also felt guilty and ugly. During my pregnancies, my family wasn't shy about telling me how worthless I was, and that I wasn't any better than my mother. That was the worst insult I could have ever received at the time. They said I was destined to be a baby making machine, having babies that my grandmother would have to take care of. I remember telling my grandmother that I couldn't wait until I was older, so I could show them otherwise. It was the only way that I knew to fight my family.

My Dark Memories started to attack me with my children, starting with the birth of my daughter. I had nightmares of being raped, and of my baby being raped. Waking up in a panic, I would strip off my daughter's diaper and check for blood. When they got old enough to understand, I taught my children the correct words for their genitalia. Instead of pee-pee and wee-wee, they would know the correct words in case someone touched them. I taught them never to sit in any man's lap, not even their uncles. This was a rule that everyone who knew my kids was supposed to abide by. I became an overprotective mom. However, I was a good mom. I played with my kids. I taught them how to read, spell, and to identify their colors and numbers. I loved the way they looked at me, as if their life couldn't get any better because they had me. That was the first time I felt unconditional LOVE. They made the Dark Memories fade.

Life got harder for me as an adult, mainly because I started making poor decisions. When I moved out of my grandmother's house, I bounced from one friend's house to another with my kids. I was addicted to marijuana and cigarettes, and I was involved in promiscuous behavior. I had never been in love, but always hoped to experience it. I remember watching TV, movies, and desiring the kind of love that I saw—the kind of love that you would kill for or die for. Love was an elusive concept for me. Because I was assaulted as a child, love was defined for me in the unhealthiest of ways.

Watching my mom in her relationships was another definition of love that I was taught. The feeling of love and the act of love were difficult for me to recognize, to reciprocate, and to be honest about. Growing up, I learned that the act of love is what you use to get what you want from men. That shaped how I defined love within a relationship. I wouldn't bring some of my boyfriends around my kids, because I didn't trust them, yet I freely gave them my body. If I did bring the guy around, I didn't know what the appropriate behavior was in the presence of my kids. I would have sex in the same room as my sleeping children rationalizing that my boyfriend couldn't mess with my children if they were right in front of me. With my Dark Memories, I lived a dual life. My mind was consumed with sex, hate, and self-loathing, but on the other hand, I had to protect my children from that part of me. In my opinion, this meant that I was fragmented, and sadly, I didn't know how to mend, heal, and become whole.

There's an old saying, "I choose the devil I know." Well, I didn't practice that. I moved out of my grandmother's house to live with friends and living with friends is a different kind of hell. When you're living with friends and can't pay rent, they own you. You're stuck babysitting all the time, while they go out and have fun. You clean up after everyone. They expect everything from you, but you can't expect anything from them. They're your friends and they love you. That love means acceptance, and it feels great, so you'll do everything they ask in order to hold on to it. Once you have no self-image, no self-esteem, and no pride, you'll accept any kind of treatment and convince yourself it's love. I felt jealousy over the littlest things, and I remember wanting to die. Surrounded by all these people, I felt lonely, worthless, and that life was not meant for me. I had no special purpose or contribution, and the worst of all; I thought that my children would have been better off without me. These Dark Memories would continue for years.

At age 23, I moved back to Grand Cayman with my children. It was a very low point in my life. That year my children changed schools seven times. The 9/11 attacks happened a few years earlier, and all my money and efforts towards getting a work visa or green card were in vain. Because I had run out of places to live, I was worried that my kids would be taken away from me. Worrying myself sick, I wondered what I would do if I saw R or T again. I knew I had to set my mother straight. Her boyfriends were never to be around my kids by themselves, or at night even with her there. I also entertained the thought that if I saw T again, I would slit his throat. I convinced myself that no one knew me there, and I could become anyone I wanted to be.

Moving back, I lived in a very small studio apartment right next door to my mother. It was great. My children loved meeting her, and I got a job within the first two weeks of being there. I paid rent and utilities, something I've never done, and I was happy.

Then, I came face-to-face with a Dark Memory. My mom said she had to pick up a new phone from a friend, and afterwards we would drive straight home. Having had a full day, my kids and I were tired and hungry. As my mom pulled into the gas station, I saw a figure with a familiar frame whose face I couldn't recognize right away. Immediately, I felt a familiar anger rise inside me.

As mom got out of the car and he turned around, I recognized and knew it was R. Everything inside me wanted to run out of the car and start beating him and her too. My kids stopped me. My son and I share a sixth sense—he always knows when something is wrong with me, no matter how hard I try to disguise or hide it. He said, "Mommy, I love you." My daughter said, "Today was fun. I'm happy we moved here." I remembered moving my hand from the door handle, but I didn't remember putting it there.

When my mom got back into the car, she saw my face, and she asked what was wrong. I warned her that if she ever brought my kids around R or T, I would never speak to her again and she would never see them again. Later, I told her what R did to me as a child. Funny thing is that she thought it was because I witnessed the beatings he used to give her. She was sincerely sorry, and I realized that perhaps she didn't know how to be a mom. I let go of the hatred and started trying to like her. I love and adore my mom today, and she has become one of my closest friends and biggest supporter.

Life was good. With every new job, I received a higher job title and more responsibility, all with a high school diploma. I lived the way I wanted, and my children were experiencing new things every day. I worked as a security guard, a tour guide, a stingray handler, a monitor for a security company, and as a department supervisor for a grocery store. When I received my first big promotion, I felt great about myself. I remember telling myself, "You did it! You're turning into a great person." The promotion was for sales, and I learned that I have the gift of gab. I could sell to anyone from any status in society.

This time of my life was very important because I began building self-esteem and I was able to discover my natural talents. I discovered that I'm artistic, creative, and whimsical. Additionally, I realized that I could use these attributes to help me with my past, and that I had been using them throughout my life to cope with the darkness. In the midst of being raped or molested, I fantasized about different worlds or about being a warrior with special powers. At school, I wrote stories with ease, page after page. I drew all the time as a way of escaping the reality of the arguments and the beatings that my mom endured. It was wonderful getting to know this part of me. Then Dark Memories.

Although I was born in Cayman, I soon discovered that I wasn't considered a Cayman citizen. When all was said and done, I spent thousands of dollars trying to rectify this problem. One way to receive status was through a maternal parent who was born in the Cayman Islands. This would be a breeze, because my father was born and bred in Grand Cayman. I had to take a paternity test and then submit the results to immigration, so they could finalize my status.

Calling my father was difficult. At age ten, my mother and I met him at a building where he would change my last name and give me $50. I resented him greatly because I attended school with his other children and they frequently shared about how much he did for them and what their weekend plans were. Secretly, I wondered why he didn't love me. Was it because I had dark skin, and the rest had light skin? Was it because I moved away, and he didn't know me? Whatever the case, I hated him for not loving me. After paying almost $400 for the test, the results were in. I couldn't understand why the nurse insisted that I come to the facility to get the results instead of telling me on the phone.

Once I arrived, the nurse told me that this man that I hated for so long was not my biological father. I spoke with him later, trying to apologize for the hate I harbored for him, and trying to explain to him why this was such a blow. I told him I understood why he neglected me, didn't protect me, or love me. I told him I understood because he knew I wasn't his. I remember looking at my birth certificate and seeing that my mother was a fifteen-year-old student and this man I thought was my father was a twenty-five-year-old police officer. I do know that he and my mom did have sexual relations when she was very young, but those encounters did not result in me. This man told me that he agreed to change my last name to his so that I could go to school, Island politics and all that. "But why claim a child you had no intentions on bringing up and no intentions on caring for. Was it because you were blackmailed?" I thought to myself. Again, fifteen-year old school girl, twenty-five year old police officer.

On the way home, I purchased a bottle of Tequila and prepared myself to confront my mother. When I shared the results with my mother, she started sobbing, saying that she didn't want me to find out. Everything inside me got very still. What in the world was she about to drop on me? Her words pierced my soul. Through red, teary eyes, she revealed that I was a product of rape. In that moment, I felt more worthless than ever. In an alcohol-induced state, it all began to make sense to me. "Of course, I came to be from a violent act. I wasn't created with love, so how could I ever be loved?" That day, I drank until I passed out.

Later, I was told that my grandmother's boyfriend raped my mom and she got pregnant and was forced to have an abortion. So out of revenge, she got pregnant with me on purpose. I don't know which story is true and I'm not sure I want to know because I have chosen to forgive. I'm sure my mom convinced herself to believe a lie told so many years before, but that lie will shape generations to come. My last name is now a man's name that has no relation to me and my son now bare this name and so will any child that comes after him. This will be a constant reminder of this darkness.

The good times kept on rolling after that. I lost my supervisory job when another company bought out the grocery store that employed me. It broke me. Everything had been going so well. I had moved into a two-bedroom apartment with my kids a year earlier, and I had gotten my first car. Now, for the first time in my life, I was dismissed from a job. I always knew I didn't take disappointment the way "normal people" did. Disappointment was life-changing for me, no matter how big or how small. As I sunk into a deep depression, I lost my home and my car, and started living with family again. Darkness engulfed me completely. My hair fell out in patches, I did the bare minimum for my kids, and I stopped caring altogether. All that I could think was, "Again? Again? Why? Will my life never be good? Will I never stop feeling pain?" After six years in Grand Cayman, I moved back to America.

My return to America was meant to get me back to a good place—a place where the darkness and Dark Memories would go away. I researched how I could get a work permit, and I just knew that it would work this time. I had the money to submit the application, and I felt that there was finally light at the end of the tunnel. We moved back just in time for my son to start high school. This meant a lot to me, as I always wanted my children to graduate from a high school in America. Because I wasn't an American, I saw all the privileges that were offered to its citizens, and I wanted to make sure my American children got every opportunity their country could offer. I wanted them to have a better life than I did. However, when I went to the immigration office, they told me that I didn't qualify for the status for which I was applying, and that they would continue to stamp my passport as a visitor as long as I have American dependents. This meant that I would not be able to work, have my own place, or own a car. I was right back where I was six years prior.

Staying with family and friends was different this time around because I knew what I would and wouldn't tolerate. Sometimes, you must tolerate being used and taken advantage of for the sake of your children, especially when you can't support yourself. At this point in my life, I had a better understanding of unconditional love and genuine goodwill. However, I started to hurt because old feelings and Dark Memories surfaced. I felt worthlessness and anger creeping back, and I didn't know how to fight them.

After bouncing around once again, I moved in with my youngest sister and her children. Living with her was pretty good. I had a place where I could fit in, and I felt useful and needed. Because she was the fun aunt, my children were happy to be around her. Inside, I was still battling depression, but I tried to smile all day to trick my mind into thinking I was happy. Marijuana became my indulgence, and before long, I was fully addicted. It was my way of coping with my depression and self-loathing. If I didn't smoke marijuana all day, I would get nauseous and jittery.

My sister and her children invited me to church, but I had no faith, love, trust, or belief in God or church people. At ages seven and eight, my children decided that they wanted to become Christians and get baptized. I never stopped them from going to church or becoming baptized, but I do remember thinking that they were wasting their time on an entity that didn't listen—an entity that says if you ask for forgiveness, He would forgive you and allow you into Heaven. I thought, "If that's the case, Heaven is not for me, because I refuse to share Heaven with the men in my past who ask for His forgiveness." I hated God for that—hated that He would make me an outcast, and that He chose them over me.

My sister and kids were watching me sink lower and lower. This was certainly not the worst time in my life. I was still more comfortable than I'd been for a while, so it was tolerable. Like clockwork, another Dark Memory returned to my life. My sister's dad moved in. At first, I ignored him. He didn't speak to me, and I didn't speak to him. Shortly after, my sister began seeing someone who took all of her attention and time, making me feel twice as lonely. My youngest sister and I are very close; she understands me and isn't afraid to correct me when needed. Her correction was always done in genuine love. Rather than feeling small or wrong, I would walk away feeling like I had learned something. Now I felt like I was losing her, and worse, I had to deal with her dad on my own.

One day while I was laying on the couch, my sister's dad started taking pictures of me. I thought nothing of it. Later, my nieces came to me saying that their grandfather was showing them the pictures and making fun of me. According to him, I was ugly and looked like a beach whale. Devastated, I felt the last little piece of happiness and self-esteem fade away. Once again, I was broken. It took me a long time to like my body, to learn what clothes complimented my body, and to like the way I looked. This man, the man that during my childhood used to belittle me and hurt my feelings, shunned me. He took me right back to my childhood alongside my Dark Memories.

In a relentless onslaught, panic attacks, nightmares, and dark thoughts began to cloud my mind. They were so intense that my son wouldn't want to go to church because he was so afraid for me. I would never have taken my own life, but I would have taken his grandfather's. Those familiar memories of hurting others and feeling powerful crept back into my mind. Not only did I think of ways that I could kill him, but I also thought of a list of people I wanted to kill as well. Those thoughts weren't merely the wishes of an angry woman—they were more of an epiphany. I was tricking myself into believing this response was the only way I would ever break free.

Though it sounds like a joke to some, I often say, "My children saved lives." They certainly saved mine. In every dark period of my life, I would always choose them. I moved out of my sister's house shortly after that, not being able to stomach her dad and quiet the noise in my head simultaneously.

I bounced around with my kids a few more times before landing at a family friend's home. Loving, caring, and giving, E had been friends with my family for years. Moving in with him was OK, but I was still battling my darkness. One day, when I felt like I was at my absolute lowest in years, I started to pray. I didn't get any divine answers or even felt better—in fact, the prayer was more of a bashing towards God. Yet, at the end of the bawling and finger pointing, I made a decision. I called my youngest sister and asked her to take me to church. It was around Thanksgiving, and I can still remember what I wore, and what the pastor preached. After the Thanksgiving lunch they served, I went home and told my sister, "I wanna try this God thing." I didn't know where or how to start, or if I would be able to walk away from certain things. I just knew that I needed a change and that this was my last hope.

At first, things were slow going. I still had a massive chip on my shoulders, and my walls of steel and iron had not been broken down. In my mind, the church people weren't kind enough, and didn't do enough to make me feel welcomed. The Sunday School class was confusing, and I didn't understand what they were talking about. When I did speak up, it sounded like I was attacking. However, I knew that this was it for me, so I sought out help. I was told to download the Bible app on my phone and pick a devotion, just to get acquainted with the Word. I did one better; I searched, "How to love God." I realized that I didn't know how to love outside of my kids and my family, so I needed to learn how to love someone I couldn't touch or see. I needed to understand more about God's love, and what it meant to have faith and trust.

Soon after, my pastor's wife and I started a relationship. I knew them from before. I used to braid their daughters' hair. The Pastor's wife did something for which I am eternally grateful. She connected me with a church member who would visit me and begin Bible studies with me. Spending time with her, I began to understand God's love and started to fall in love with Him. I accepted Jesus Christ into my heart and soul, asked Him for forgiveness, and dedicated my life to being Christlike. I was baptized soon afterwards.

My Pastor, his wife, and their three daughters took my kids and me in. The Lord placed me in an environment where my children and I could see what a healthy family looked like. We observed how they lived together, worshipped together, and solved conflicts and hurts. The first time I saw them all doing their part to set the dinner table was amazing. I couldn't believe that people really did that, and that they did this every night. In speaking with my kids, they expressed how they loved being at the dinner table that way.

I quit smoking marijuana and cigarettes, and I learned how to pray. Best of all, I started to heal. Getting baptized was the most important day of my life. Some people wonder how I could choose my baptism day over my children's birthdays. On the day of my baptism, I was buried under the water allowing the old me, and the darkness inside to die. As I emerged from the water, I was being raised up out of the shadows of death, just like Jesus did. Now, I can truly appreciate the births of my children, and see them as miracles.

When I chose Him, I was able to forgive and let go, making the Dark Memories die. When they started dying, my heart and soul began to heal. When I gave myself completely to God, there was no longer room for all the hurt, torment, and darkness—that space was His, and His alone. On my "dipping day," as I call my baptism, I was so excited. I was already saved, but I wanted to do this to show my Lord that I was all in for the rest of my life.

My sister read my testimony to the congregation. Everyone teared up, and my sister could barely get through the written words. My pastor and I teared up along with them. The water was so cold. After being submerged, brought back up, and changing into fresh clothes, I was overwhelmed by a sense of calmness. I felt nothing but the presence of God. It wasn't a hand on my shoulder or a voice from the heavens, but an undeniable feeling of peace and comfort. It was everything I had ever wanted.

My memories, dark or light, will always be with me, as they are a part of me. But they will no longer control me. This involves hard work, and making a conscious effort, sometimes every minute of every day work. I still have hard times. The difference is that I know who I am, I know my worth, I know true love, and I know the compromises that I will not make. God's presence has helped me to view my hard times and hurts differently than before. I'm more confident in the way I handle myself and others, and I am more secure in my decisions because they have been guided by Him. Although they would have crushed me in previous times, my hurts and disappointments are now manageable. These memories, all of them, including the bad ones, are precious because they are a part of who I was, who I am now, and who I want to be.

# MORE ABOUT THE AUTHOR

Purpose, Passion, and Leadership are the three words 36-year-old Grand Caymanian, Robinette Rankin lives by. Robinette is a manager and volunteer coordinator for a Transitional Home for homeless women and children. She has dedicated her life to serving women— those battling depression and survivors of domestic violence.

Robinette is a certified life coach and mentor leader. She uses what she learned from the "School of Hard Knocks" as a testimony and teaching guide to uplift, inspire, and empower women to see their true potential and help them to reach their success.

Robinette is a mother of two college-attending, young adults. She credits her children with teaching her the valuable concepts of unconditional love, respect, and kindness. She believes it is important to share those attributes with everyone she encounters.

Robinette considers her grandest accomplishment as being the moment she gave her life to the Lord. It was at that moment when she began to walk and live in the purpose He intended for her life.

# Story Four

# GOD ALWAYS DELIVERS

Quietly and confidently, I often reflect, "If God calls me home today or tomorrow, I can truly say that I've lived a good life. He has never failed me, ever. His love and his presence have always been there." God's presence, through every adversity, and through every season, has truly been the source of my strength. I have seen God's hand at work, solving all my problems. Yet, I am careful to emphasize that God expects certain things from us.

During my career, I held many different jobs, mostly in retail management. As with all retail jobs, the hours were long, there were stressful periods, and of course, there were many personalities with which to get acclimated. Over the years, many challenges arose. I was given an extra workload, and I was overlooked for a fair pay raise. I recall a time when I was passed over for a promotion. I admit that at first I was disappointed, then my disappointment turned to anger towards my supervisor. Through that experience, God forced me to take a good look at myself. Despite the aggravation and frustration, I believe Christians must exemplify Christ in the workplace. We must have a Christlike attitude and not get down on the same level as our co-workers or supervisors. Realizing that this was what God expected of me, I continued to do my work diligently and faithfully.

During the 1980s, I worked as the only black female assistant manager for a company. My four male co-workers each started off making more money than I did. When the time for raises approached, I optimistically expected that my earnings would be comparable to theirs. Yet, despite the fact that two of them had less experience than me, they received higher pay raises than I did. I admit those things put me in a position to grow closer to God. I couldn't rely on myself — just the Holy Spirit, and God's strength. With that knowledge, I continued to work to the best of my ability.

A constant source of encouragement for me has been Romans 8:28, "And we know that in all things God works for the good of those who love him, who have been called according to his purpose." I am a living testimony that God really does work everything out for the good of those who love and trust him.

For several years, I worked at a large retail store. Little did I know that despite my challenges in the workplace, God was using my tenure there for something much bigger. In the late 80's, while working at the Book Department in Belk's, I met the man who would become my second husband. Coming in to buy a Bible, George initiated a conversation with me, and from that point we began talking on the phone. George was saved and was a very godly man. At that time, I admit that I wasn't following the Lord like I was supposed to. As a Bible study leader, George would call me, and we would read Bible verses together or have mini Bible studies. I acknowledge that George was placed in my life to help me develop a closer relationship with God. As one thing led to another, we began dating, and eventually got married. After getting married, later George became a minister.

Although I excelled at my job and was eventually offered the position of Store Manager, the workload at the retail store was demanding. The Layaway Department required not only 10 – 12-hour shifts, but my duties also involved late-night alarm calls, requiring me to return to the store and reset the alarm. George didn't think it was safe for me to go out alone, so he would accompany me, even if it was 1 or 2 a.m. George was a firm believer that a man should provide for and protect his family.

Because George was a minister and traveled to different churches, oftentimes, I couldn't accompany him. At times, this made George irritable because he valued the traditional custom that wives should be with their husbands. In addition to working at the store, my job required me to make out-of-town trips to help set up new stores as well. Having a demanding job was the biggest struggle we faced in our marriage. George would often tell me that he would be glad when I give up that job and become his full-time wife. He had greater dreams— namely, opening our very own Christian bookstore. Together, we sought out help from someone who could help us with our business plan for the bookstore.

While I simultaneously maintained this hectic schedule and was finishing up a computer course, George fell ill. God gave me the strength, and I did everything that I could to manage my work schedule. My sister-in-law from Philadelphia came to help me. I worked during the day, and she would spend time in the hospital with George. Eventually, I decreased my work hours and requested a leave of absence from my job. However, in June 1993, the Lord called George home, before my leave of absence was granted. It was a difficult time. Unwilling to return to the retail store immediately, I took a year and a half off when my leave of absence was finally granted. I used that time to do ministry and evangelistic work. With a more open schedule, I visited those who were hospitalized, sick, and shut-in. Making those visits allowed me to take my mind off myself. I felt it was a blessing to help someone else.

Around the time that George passed away, a fellow church member lost her husband as well. Not long afterwards, a friend from another church was widowed as well. The Lord placed it on my heart to start a support group for other widows. This was what gave birth to a ministry called Sisters in Christ, which met monthly for Bible study and encouragement. When we met, we discussed the problems we faced as widows, such as financial challenges and the upkeep of our homes. There were many things that our husbands had been doing, which left a tangible void in our lives. For example, we had a man come in to show us how to do basic car maintenance and teach us how to change a tire. Without a doubt, studying the Word together gave us the most comfort. This group met for three years and even grew to include women who were unmarried. After three years, I stopped leading the group, as God had not prompted me to continue the ministry. When a friend approached me about continuing the group, I encouraged her to pray about it and see if the Lord was leading her to continue the ministry.

Despite my unwavering assurance of God's presence with me, I knew it was time to do something else. I was lonely for human companionship, and I couldn't stay in the house for another year and a half, by myself, at night. My three sons from a previous marriage were grown and on their own. I knew that getting back out of the house was also a part of the healing process. Choosing not to return to the retail store, I chose a job where I could instead work the graveyard shift. I started out as a regular employee and became a supervisor five years later.

During this season, God prompted me that it was time to pursue George's dream of opening a Christian bookstore. I believe God taught me the skills needed to establish the bookstore from my former retail store experiences. While I was in the retailer's Store-Within-a-Store program, I was responsible for 14 departments and seven managers. I learned how to merchandise, do Profit and Loss (P & L) statements, payroll, and displays. Because of the skills I learned, I eventually hired two people for my bookstore.

In order to open the Christian bookstore, I needed to find a suitable location. I started looking in Downtown Columbia, near the State Capitol. Only God could orchestrate what happened next. The Baptist Bookstore, also located downtown at the time, was moving to the Harbison area. As a result, I was able to acquire most of their shelving and displays to furnish my store. I was amazed at how God was at work. I named the bookstore, The Little Vessel. That name stood out to me years before, when I saw it on a van.

With the unwavering support of my pastor and church family, and with shelves full of books, The Little Vessel opened its doors in 1994. We were open for 5 ½ days each week and had about 25-30 customers each week. Through its 10 years of operation, and many ups and downs, I continued to see God's hand at work. At the two-year mark, sales were slow, and I became discouraged and thought about closing the store. The Lord was providing, but I was expecting more. The Holy Spirit reminded me that God wanted people downtown to have a place where they could come for Christian literature and music. I had to come to grips with the fact that God would provide for all of my needs. God reminded me that He didn't put me there to fail, and that the store was a ministry to the people who walked through its doors. As I headed to the bank to make a deposit, I found a metered parking space right outside. Just as I was about to put my money into the meter, my eyes fell on a roll of money neatly placed before my front tire. I believed that God meant the money for me.

On another occasion, while I was looking through the door, a tall, white male walked into the store. Being well dressed, with blonde hair, he looked much like the typical customer, with the exception of two things — he was extremely tall, and his face was unlike any I had seen before. This man's face was really shining, like a glow. However, he did not have a smile on his face. We exchanged greetings, and then he asked me if I had any books on angels. I guided him to the section that contained books about angels, and he chose a book to purchase. After completing his purchase, he headed for the door. Instantly, I had the urge to see where he was going. As I ran to the front door, I looked to the left, to the right, and across the street. He had vanished. It didn't dawn on me, until after he had left, that I came face-to-face with an angel. I know that God sent that angel to remind me that He was watching over me.

On yet another day, I was sitting on my stool whining and complaining because I only had one or two customers that day. Shortly thereafter, a lady entered the store and said, "The Lord told me to tell you that this place is a blessing." She then proceeded to walk through the store praising God and speaking blessings over The Little Vessel. It was unreal, I recall. I felt the need to repent, because God had already said that he would provide. I never saw that woman again.

Story upon story of God's presence at The Little Vessel delights and warms my heart to this day. In downtown Columbia, there were many who were homeless for a variety of reasons. Some had fallen on hard times, some were addicts, some were uneducated, etc. I fondly remember the time when I met a young, hungry, homeless man at the store. I took him next door to buy him a meal, and I witnessed to him, because he did not know the Lord. My priority was to give him a meal first, because if a person is hungry or needs clothes, it's hard to witness to them without those needs being met. Two years later, he returned to thank me, and let me know that he had given his life to Christ. It was an awesome experience.

In fact, over the years, many people came into the store to tell me how the store was an encouragement to them. Because there were a lot of homeless people in the area, I would often let them come into The Little Vessel when there were terrible thunderstorms and rain. It was like a haven for them. They began to come every day, even when there wasn't a storm. I gave them some money when they asked, but soon learned that giving money was not always the best method. There was a time when I gave a homeless man some money, and later learned that he took that money and went to the liquor store. Despite my discouragement, I was still convicted that is was my duty to help the poor according to Proverbs 21:13. After this, I would offer to buy them a sandwich or something else to eat instead of just giving them money. With confidence, I believe God had that store there for a reason.

As I reflect on my life, I often brim with excitement. God has been so good to me. He has kept me, protected me, and been there for me. I still have trouble believing some of the wonderful things that have taken place since my husband passed away. God is so faithful, even when we are unfaithful and ungrateful. He is a loving, caring, and a good God. The Bible talks about the importance of thanksgiving and prayer, and I am particularly struck by the importance of prayer. It brings us into the presence of God, it gives us a chance to talk to God, and give thanks for what He's done and is doing. Prayer gives us a chance to open the door of our hearts and listen to God. He gives us the strength and the wisdom we need if we seek Him with a sincere heart. We need to learn to put our faith to work. God expects things of us, and we have to do our part.

## MORE ABOUT THE AUTHOR

Delores Brown is a strong woman of faith. She has always had an entrepreneurial spirit. Mrs. Brown is a former business owner and manager to a Christian Bookstore, "The Little Vessel" for ten years.

She received her Bachelor's of Science Degree in Business Administration from the University of South Carolina in Columbia, SC.

Delores is very people-oriented. For years, she has been actively advocating to ensure people use their voice to shape the political system by their vote. She has worked at polls during elections.

Delores has a passion to serve the elderly population and work in evangelism.

Some of her hobbies include designing, flower arrangements, and art collecting.

Delores is a widow and the mother of three grown sons Gregory, Jimmie, and Derek.

# Story Five

# AIN' NOBODY TOLD ME IT WAS ABUSE

When you are a child, you only have the authority to eat, play, and sleep. Growing up in the south in the 50's, you did what you were told (if you were not rebellious). My surrogate mother had me bound and gagged in my mind. But as a child, I didn't entirely know that. I, for the most part, thought I was like any other child in my neighborhood, church, and school. I had a quiet older brother, who typically could have been my dad. He married at 29 when I was four. I lived as an only child to a two-parent household with a dog, parakeet, and fish aquarium. Things seemed so normal. But sharp phrases would catch me off guard, like *"I treat you better than my own son"* coupled with, *"you get more than any child 'round here"* or *"you ain' nothing, and yo' mama before you wasn't nothing."* I didn't know it was abuse because ain' nobody told me it was abuse. That crazy saying of *"Words will never hurt me"* was obviously spoken by an absent-hearted person, because that statement has NEVER been true. Every insult, every degrading mockery, and every manipulating rule hurt more than any fist or strap could ever. At least those surface scars healed quickly and naturally.

Before I discovered I was an alien implanted in the Merritts' family, I was a happy-go-lucky child with no worries, except little absences called Epilepsy. When I was 25 years old, my mama received a letter from the Department of Social Services. It had a picture of them, as they were *grooming* to be my parents in their early 50's. The letter was talking about changing their system from paper files to microfiche. The letter spoke of a baby. Of course, I jumped to conclusions, thinking my parents had the itch to adopt another kid. There's no way in HELL I was going to let that happen. In fact, I said in no uncertain terms, "OH, NO MA'AM! You will NOT be adopting any more children. You can't put another child through what you put me through!" Mama looked at me sideways and said, "You done lost your mind. I ain' trying to adopt no baby!" When I heard her admit that she couldn't or wouldn't take on that responsibility again, then I slowed all the way down to actually read the letter. It was indeed talking about a baby – with my birthdate and year. But one thing that differed was the name: Baby Juanita was the name on the letter. Then I had the whole fact. The letter was about me, and these half century parents wanted to adopt a little baby girl. I was the baby; I was baby Juanita.

Digging a little further with permission from my mother who told me when I inquired to learn more about my own family, "If you old enough to ask, you old enough to know." Because of health issues and having a son with Down's Syndrome, I thought this would answer all my questions: Who am I? Where did I come from? Why am I here? How did I get here? What will become of me?

I learned that my orphanage name was Ethel Lazarus. Then my adopted parents amended my name to Louise Marie. This sweet little perfect-seeing little girl became a sad and ugly, broken, and self-loathing teen and young adult. I remember the day my mama told me about the cookies in the cookie jar. I didn't know at that time she was breaking me, manipulating me, and degrading me.

Let me interject for all parents. We do have the power over our young children to steer them in the right direction. The Holy Bible isn't a book of suggestions, rather a book of instruction and training. **Proverbs 22:6** is clear in the message that we train up a child in the way he should go, and when he is old he will not depart from the principles of that training. The Scriptures also speak to the responsibility of parents on integrity and character. There are parents who go too far with insults, discipline, discouragement, and punishment. **Ephesians 6:4** and **Colossians 3:21** both remind fathers [parents] not to provoke their children to wrath [anger], lest they be discouraged, but to bring them up in the nurture and admonition of the Lord.

Back to the '*cookie jar story.*' Mama and I went to the market called Big Star Grocery. She ordered a large list of groceries as she commonly did every other week. We walked every aisle picking up food, nonperishables, and some fun things, or let's just call them rewards for just being at the store. When we returned home, she turned the key off to the ignition switch on our beautiful red and white 52' Chevy with the comfy white seats that I loved. She used the same key ring to open the trunk. There it was...a trunk full of neatly creased, brown paper bags filled with groceries. Mama and I made a path from the trunk to the front door stairs all the way through to the kitchen with the groceries. We walked a few good times before finally putting all the bags in the house. Once we were done, our final march to the vehicle was to close the trunk.

In this moment, I felt good about our 'Mother & Daughter' relationship. I felt I was fulfilling the golden rule learned in

Sunday School, "Do unto others as you have them do unto you." I felt great because I sensed that she was liking me. I was feeling some kind of happy because I was sharing a moment with my beautiful mother. I wanted that feeling to go on forever. Most times, I was not so fortunate. I was careful to put away the sugar and rice sacks, the milk in the fridge, and the great number of canned goods. I also put away the washing powder and the bars of soap, while my mama focused on separating the meats, vegetables, and bagging them for the freezer. After her task was over, I waited for that special thing she would do with the snacks. The Little Debbie Raisin Creme Pies, cheese balls, and coconut cookies were our usual goodies. The snacks were added to the daily lunch for the family. They were compartmentalized in certain jars and drawers, with the exception of the ice cream and the coconut cookies. The cookies, which were my absolute favorite, were always accessible in a heavy lead crystal cookie jar.

On grocery days when mama would sing while cutting up the meat and putting away the groceries, it was a good indication she was in a good mood. I just knew I was going to get a Dixie cup full of cheese balls or a paper towel with three cookies, along with a Dixie paper cup filled with milk. Everything must be perfect from my perspective. I needed to be sure everything would be in its place, no awkward movements, only smiles with just the right amount of questions or answers, and the best behavior with the finest niceties!

Things were going perfectly when suddenly, the worst fear happened. While humming one of her favorite church songs, my mama turned and looked at me as if she'd never seen me before and said, "Dees cookies I'm 'bout to put in dis here cookie jar has already been counted. You can only git two cookies and if you git more than that, I'll know it, and you'll be beaten with many stripes." You talk about scared of my mama? I was more scared of her than I was of God. I only ate the cookies she gave me.

All kinds of thoughts started coming to my mind. What if she forgot the count? What if one of the cookies broke in my favorite crystal cookie jar? I was already getting my share of beatings a day. I was not trying to add anything other to my plight. I got a whippin' for being clumsy, talking to myself (my imaginary friends), walking grown, having emotions, rocking back and forth on my knees, and looking in her direction when she's talking to an adult. There were so many rules to keep up with. I call them fencing rules – rules made up as you go. As a child, you just knew that you would get punished for breaking these ever-changing, unspoken rules. Now that I'm an adult, I see how we have the upper hand. There's no way one could instantly know these rules as a child. Usually, my education would come in the slap, knock, brush, shoe, extension cord, or from her iron fist.

Mama was very devout and as she put it, "I'mma upstanding Christian woman in this community and ain' nobody can spot my life." Living holy and set apart meant something to black folks born in the late 1800's – through the early 1900's, because they had nothing else of their own. Their lives had been snatched, stolen, and upstaged by white folks for centuries. They had to learn to bow down in order to live. Coloreds were not stupid; they saw how life worked; and they brought some of those ungodly practices into their own shanties and shacks. For generations, demeaning and degrading mentality grew in our culture.

My parents were both saved, sanctified, and filled up with the Holy Ghost, on their way to Heaven, and enjoying the trip. Yes, mother would be loving on Jesus with everything within her and she taught me to love HIM too. I once heard a man say, "She's doing all she knows to do; she just doesn't know much." This is a classic explanation of those raised in the dark age of slavery and degradation. My dad was a more gentler soul. He was not much on the rod of correction; but he did believe in discipline. However, he gave life nuggets, of which I am still using today. He learned how to love and to tolerate his wife's insecurities, meanness, and bossiness. At times, she was like a volcano waiting to erupt. On the flip side of my mama's rough side, was a smooth skinned, long black haired, big hipped, and redbone descent of Cherokee Indian who loved nice things, nice clothes, and she could cook you into a fit. Everybody loved her mouth-watering dishes. Lord, that woman could cook!

Behind closed doors, there was a distinct difference in how mama acted when she was at home. She was more refined as an upstanding Christian at work and church. Sometimes, I would often wonder if she was nicer when I wasn't in proximity to do something to mess it all up. My whole life I felt like I was always putting out 200% just to get 50% back from her. There is a Good Book quote I considered a rule. It says, "Cast thy bread upon the waters: for thou shalt find it after many days." This simply means do good, and good will come back to you. That rule didn't always work for me with mama.

But in defense of my beautiful mother, she made sure I

looked my best with the finest clothes she and my dad could buy, toys galore, electronics, musical instruments, anything that a child could have, I had it. That was so wonderful; especially when I got to share it with cousins or an occasional visitor. I definitely had things—beautiful clothes and hairstyles; but I never had her. On one hand, I felt she was proud of me because I sang and played the piano, I was crowned Miss Black Florence 1974, and even though I had a learning challenge, I graduated high school and had some college courses. On the other hand, I felt she was ashamed of me because of the many illnesses I was diagnosed with. I believe mama didn't want me to be a spectacle, because she didn't want to be judged for choosing a sickly little girl.

There are so many stories about the spirit of my mother's demons. Clearly, her dysfunction turned us dysfunctional. My brother was a silent alcoholic; and I became suicidal, nervous, and depressed. The doctors said I was manic depressive. My mother always contended that she was NOT the crazy one; I was. She said I was crazy because I had epileptic seizures (petit mal, grand mal, and Jacksonian). She referred to the convulsions as fits. I also suffered greatly with migraines and asthma. The inability to breathe was so intense. There were days while trying to breathe in and out from a tight chest, I would lay down because of exhaustion from trying to gasp for air. When I tried to inhale or exhale, the bed would literally shake. Mama's love was genuine, though to some, it seemed warped. She didn't want me to suffer, so she would try little home remedies.

I'm going to warn you in advance that what I'm about to share is graphic, uncensored, and may make you barf, but it is what I experienced. There were days when breathing was such a chore. My mama would draw a bath of cool water and use a washcloth to pour over my body, then rub my chest down with Vicks Vapor Rub and put me to bed under a heap of blankets to help me sweat the asthma out. But this night was different. On this evening, while I soaked, mama left my side to get a bathroom style Dixie cup. She gave the cup to me and had me to excrete in it, then told me to drink that warm bile excrement. I felt some kind of way, but the compassion in her eyes made me trust her decision. Neither one of us liked the onslaught and effects of asthma. From a child's perspective, I was thinking, "It came from me, so how could it NOT be good for me, right? My mama loves me and wants me well, so this could work out." The color was similar to the color of a Mountain Dew, so I wasn't expecting the bitter, foul taste. Warm drinks were usually inviting, like the good feeling when you drink warm milk or warm tea. However, after that sip, I looked at my mama in shock. It was nasty! She said, "Drink it! Drink it all down! It'll cut dat asthma. You don't want dat asthma, do you?" I shook my head hard and fast while trying to ingest it with a despicable look on my face and the despicable taste going down my throat. I believe she thought she was helping. But ain' nobody told her it was abuse.

At the direction of an old preacher, mama, by the grace of God, used healing olive oil to coat my flesh after casting the devil out of me. She first opened a clothes hanger and put it on top of the stove. When it was red hot on the ends, she pricked me all over my skin. I squirmed between her legs because of the heat. Mama demanded I take it because it was going to help me. She prayed, "Come out in the name of Jesus, you foul devil!" The experience seemed awful for us both. Nonetheless, her maternal desires to have me be well took her to great measures outside the normal limits. Mama took the olive oil and prayed, "Heal my child, Low'd, heal my child." She rubbed me ever so tenderly, helped me with my pajamas, and I went to bed thinking I was going to be cured from all my illnesses. She believed. So, I believed because she did it all in the name of Jesus. I didn't know it was wrong; because ain' nobody told me it was abuse.

I suffered vascular migraines. To me, the pain of the headaches was just as bad as the three types of seizures I lived with. The doctor told my mama I needed shock treatments. At twelve years old, I had to go every other week for almost a year. It was one of the most horrid experiences of my childhood. I had to go to the room where the upside-down flip gurney was located. I had to have straps at my feet, legs, chest, and head for the 15-minute plug-up shock treatments, just so I could be called normal. I am so glad that shock treatments were banned in the mid 1970's. I was diagnosed with having mania; renamed the modern-day bi-polar disorder. Alongside all the shock treatments, I had to take that nasty medicine called Ritalin syrup, coupled with Dilantin, Phenobarbital, and Sinequan. I was a straight up medicinal zombie.

Even though I had epileptic seizures, these clinicians would induce the "fits" to make me better. What? That's an oxymoron. The doctors told my parents I was not normal, so to justify their science, they hooked my head up to the strangest apparatus, put metal-like leads (resembling a tuning fork) in my mouth and flipped me upside down, so I wouldn't choke from the foaming saliva from my mouth. All that for normalcy? It's a wonder that I have any live cells in my brain, or cognitive skills to think and put things together. I recall crying and telling my dad I didn't want to go through the shock treatments anymore. My dad wiped my tears and said to me in his tenderest voice, "You know what *nomial* (his pronunciation for normal) is? It's the setting on a washing machine. *Nomial* is where you are and what you do at the moment." That made me feel so amazing. Not too many months after my dad's encouragement, a law was passed to ban shock treatments. By thirteen years old, I didn't have to deal with the anguish, fear, and inhumane treatment that went along with shock treatments. What a phenomenal birthday present for me! HAPPY BIRTHDAY!

I had old parents, and they "chose" me to be their child. According to mama, I was sickly, ugly, and nobody wanted me. She often said I was nothing and my mama before me was nothing. WOW! What a statement. To me, that was a completely off the wall remark. I tried to put it all together in my head what she was saying. "But, aren't you my mother?" I asked. Before 12 years of age, I didn't know what that statement meant, yet I heard it multiple times a week.

The Saturday morning my mama told me I was adopted was a day that I wish I could forget. I was crushed and confused. I was 12 years old. She said so many negative things that day, but the ones that seared me the most was that no one wanted me, and I was going to wind up an orphan, but she came along and "rescued" me. So, I should be thankful, she suggested. If it weren't for her, I wouldn't be here or anywhere she told me. This was the day I succumbed to my emotions and DIED. My teachers didn't seem to like me, my peers didn't seem to like me, my mama's birth son and his wife didn't seem to like me—

so nothing mattered. I tuned all the bad feelings out of my mind and walked around numb just to survive. My soul was so bruised and battered, year after year, from verbal, emotional, and physical cruelty. The one person who advocated for me and stood up for me was a Godly man who loved me with all his might. But his love, my mama thought, was a cloak for me, and she didn't like it one bit. She hated my relationship with most people and said things like, 'Stop being so happy. You just too happy.' Another horrible quote of mama was, "Stop speaking to people you don't know. Why you always speaking to *mens*? You just man-struck." What did that mean? I didn't know at 9 or 10 years old what that could mean, but it didn't feel like it was a compliment. It was like a hate gene took over mama's thoughts and soul. Here comes another one of those fencing rules. "I want you to stop kissing your daddy goodnight." That's right, she forbade me to say I love you to him, hug, or kiss him goodnight, or show any type of affection. When she said to me, "I want you to stop kissing and licking up on your daddy. That don't look good," I was in the first grade. I was very inquisitive until my curiosities were dulled by, you guessed it, mama. I asked my mama, why did I have to stop saying I love you to my daddy.

In my mind as a young child not older than six or seven, I concluded that my daddy and my mama were both the same; they were my parents. Unfortunately, mama didn't have the answer I could appreciate. She simply said, "Did you hear what I said? It don't look good. Don't tell a man you love him. He'll do what he wants to do to you. I bet not ever hear talk of you saying that or doing that. You hear me?" I had to say, "Yes ma'am," but without understanding. My dad in his wisdom uttered not a word, but the love we shared as parent and daughter was ever-present though unspoken. I trusted my dad, so I went with mama's rule.

One day my dad became gravely ill. The ambulance came to carry him to the hospital. We lived several blocks from the downtown infirmary. When I heard about my daddy, adrenalin took over and I ran as fast as my feet would move all the way to the hospital. I was out of breath, but when I saw my daddy, who for as long as I could remember never had one hospital emergency, or hospital stay for himself. I was terrified my daddy was going to die. So, I took courage. I went past all the tumultuous screams in my confused head from my mama's forbidden words. I said to my daddy in a panicked and thunderous voice, pushing and forcing it until the first sentence was exposed, "DADDY, I LOVE YOU! DON'T DIE DADDY. I WILL NEVER STOP SAYING I LOVE YOU. I DON'T CARE WHO TELLS ME TO STOP. I WILL NEVER STOP SAYING I LOVE YOU. I LOVE YOU. I LOVE YOU. I LOVE YOU! YOU CAN'T DIE DADDY. I LOVE YOU AND I WANT YOU TO LIVE." Then I kissed him all over his head, face, and hands. My emotions broke. I felt a release from my bowels. It was insurmountable. It was love! I was free, and my daddy's face lit up as if I was the most famous person he had ever seen. He was free to say to me, "I love you, too!"

The silent struggles and pain I carried (because you'd better not speak what goes on in the house) was soothed by going to church hearing the great rhythmic and joyful songs, hearing the emotional talks from the young and old Christians, and watching people, even my mama shout (thinking that God, her Father, was beating her for beating me). I would cry and sing.

Going to church was so inspirational; I was impressed and lifted by the rhythms, melodies, and emotions. When I was four years of age, I distinctly remember banging on any flat surface as if it were a musical instrument. WHEN GOD GAVE ME MUSIC, it literally saved my life. I would sing every day—whether I had a piano or not. The music was my salvation, and the gospel music was my blues. With emotional turmoil and confusion in my soul and sickness in my body, I thought everybody was like this. I thought all mamas and daddies were nice, of God, and everything was normal, because ain' nobody told me I was abused.

Time didn't wait for me. I was turning into a young lady, and I didn't know about life outside the grocery store, school, church, and my parents' home. I was quite comfortable playing with my dolls and tea sets, writing songs, singing, playing the piano, or writing poetry. I wasn't much on television, except a few black T.V. shows. But, my absolute favorite show was Medical Center (M.C.). This show aired Monday nights at 8 o'clock.

On one particular night, my mama sent me to bed early as a punishment because of something dumb I did. This night I was willing to have taken a beating in exchange to stay up for Dr. Joe Gannon, who was the handsomest blue-eyed man I had ever seen. I couldn't miss the opportunity to see the show. I went to bed crying. I was silently hoping to hear something from the show. But, that didn't happen. I believe my mama turned the volume on the T.V. down on purpose. I thought to myself, "I'll make up my own show, I will be famous for my show and then I'll be able to watch M.C. whenever I want to." So, I began to carve out a plot on which to write my screenplay.

I was hooked on finishing it so much so until I took my typewriter to school.

My peers were inquisitive about my work. Some of my classmates started reading a few of the pages I had written. They made positive comments and pressed me for more pages each day. The teacher got involved, and she let it get in the hands of the principal and his secretary. They helped me to go further. They didn't stop until my story was aired as a part of the Medical Center's 1971 series. Several people edited my script, but I was credited as one of the writers. I was offered an opportunity for a college scholarship upon graduation to the University of Southern California, with a concentration in creative writing. Of course, my family didn't understand my creative side. Mama gave me no support. She said I would never leave the city because I was too sickly with fits. She thought nobody needed the responsibility of my care. It was her burden. So, I continued writing and singing to myself and the LORD. Everywhere I went, I would soothe myself with a song. The arts were my only friends, because the arts were true. We completely understood each other.

I don't know if holding me back from the things I liked, such as sports (track), music, going to college, and creation on every medium was considered abuse. I believe she genuinely didn't want me to be exposed to strangers in another state on the west side of the United States. Nevertheless, it is always unusually cruel, in my opinion, to squash someone's dreams.

Some of the greatest events of mama and my relationship were far and few between, but this was one of my all-time favorites. My mama had a fetish for pretty things, such as pitchers and goblet sets. She had many tea sets and pitcher sets. She took me one day to an antique store. Her eyes fell on this antique blue 5-piece goblet and pitcher set. She asked my opinion, and I responded according to its beauty. Mama made the purchase. The clerk took her time and wrapped each goblet and placed it in a brown paper bag with a strong, paper rope handle. Mama was careful carrying it to the car. When we got home, she filled up the sink with hot water, got a little bleach and dish detergent to carefully wash the set in preparation for its new home. She then displayed her new trophies in the china cabinet.

The pastor of my mama's church came for an occasional dinner with a few other guests. Not to my surprise, one of the centerpieces was the blue pitcher. Later that year, I was going to be turning 13. I slipped into my courage enough to ask if we could have a party using the heavy antique blue 5-piece pitcher and goblet set. I wanted that feeling of specialness as I poured out my favorite grape flavored Kool-Aid beverage. I was shocked when mama said, "Yes," and I'm sure she was equally as shocked when I asked.

Six years later, when I was 19, I did the DUM-DUM-DEE-DUMB thing. Yes, I went on the word of my mother and married the man she coerced me to marry (her being in fear I would be an old maid). I didn't know him longer than a New York minute. We met at college, and he chased and pursued me. Although we courted 2 days a week for six months, I had no inkling of what life was actually like. We spent time together. I met his family, he went with me to church a few times, we talked over the phone, and saw each other on campus. But, in my opinion, it wasn't enough to say, I do. We knew nothing about each other. If you don't know what a thing is or who someone is, you are most likely or liable to get entangled with it repeatedly. We had simple blow-ups and we kissed a lot. When he asked me for my most sacred gift, I told him, "Until you say I do, I won't!" My mama and the church taught us not to commit adultery or fornication. In essence, "keep your drawers up and your dress down, and you won't have a baby."

When we got married, mama purchased and upgraded her furniture and gave me the pieces I was familiar with. Mama told me to choose what I wanted in the house. She obliged many of my choices. That was so special. I chose the heavy oak rocking chair. She gave me the bedroom set I carved my alphabets in as a youngster, and many other cosmetic things like curtains, tablecloths, sheets, etc. I felt so loved and special 'till I went a little further. I was feeling froggy on that instance by asking for her silver tea server. Obviously, I had crossed the line. "You can forget that. You ain't gonna have my tea server," she said matter-of-factly. That being said, I figured it would be of no use to ask about the blue antique pitcher and goblet set from my 13th birthday celebration. I was very happy about my new pieces for our new home with my new husband.

On Christmas 1977, my mom gave me a gift wrapped present. It was a big package; heavy too. I tore into it with anticipation and excitement only to discover the five-piece blue antique pitcher and goblet set. That was my Christmas gift. I felt ultimate joy. I sensed my mama knew how much that meant to me. Maybe that was her plan all the time, but what was certain, the set was passed down to me! I was joyous about this gift from her at such a pivotal time in my life.

The institution of marriage and the institution of parenthood are supposed to be the ultimate joy. I was in love with the idea of being in love and being a mother. One of my good friends told me after 8 years of marriage, "Louise, you know you're not happy." I was appalled, but what was true was that I had tricked myself into thinking I was happy, as a coping mechanism. I think I hid from my own self. I was in denial—the cuss-outs, the lack of money, the beatings, the threats with guns, the many nights alone as he made drug runs.

Now my former husband didn't have a cake walk with me either as his wife. He had to contend with my depression, the lack of not knowing my birth family, my loneliness, the mental and physical illnesses, and three children—on top of all the other issues, a special needs child. At first, I ran to music for help; and he ran to drugs and alcohol for help. But, as life became more problematic, I started having extramarital affairs, and he turned to more drugs, violence, and alcohol just to cope. I had absolutely no self-worth, so I went deeper into loathing by masturbation, mutilation, and kleptomania. The more mentally sick I was, the more the symptoms plagued me.

The day I thought I would die was the Sunday I fell on the porch of my home with a grand malfunction in my brain. The hospital report said I had about 20 seizures. I was unconscious for many days. I was also pregnant with our youngest son, K. My body died and was revived. But, I was mad because I wasn't doing well, and I wanted to go where Jesus was, since I could get no real healing for my body and mind. I couldn't believe that for the two times I tried to commit suicide in my youth, none of the attempts worked. I was a reject from the portals of

Heaven's gates. I tried overdosing on Phenobarbital and Sinequan. Death seemed much better than what I was in. Wow, it seemed that even God didn't want me. But in a loving instant, God spoke to my spirit and said He couldn't take me because I had to finish my assignment. My first assignment was motherhood. I needed my children and they needed me. I cried, begged, and pleaded just to see His face. He was adamant. In fact, he spoke no more about it.

When K was born, the doctors had already given us a grim outlook. Because he lost a lot of oxygen, the doctors believed he could even be stillborn. But, that wasn't what happened. When he came out of me, he was another perfect being from the imagination of God. He weighed 6 lbs., 2 oz., and 18 inches long, with slanted eyes. The doctors told me to put my child in a home, because he was a Mongoloid child. "He has the Down's Syndrome, and he will be mentally retarded. It will be difficult raising him with your other children," they told me. I was very firm with Dr. Price, "I AM gonna put him in a home; MY HOME! That's my child!"

Having my children were the best events that EVER happened to me. We loved each other as if each one of us were GOD. Our relationship as a young mother to my children and vice versa was perfect. There was NO condition to our love. It was AGAPE! Although there were health challenges, lack of money, food, essential things, lack of a dad/husband, we made it quite successfully even through the intellectual challenges. K was not the only one riding that train; we all had challenges in that arena. The acceptance of a slightly less than perfect child sent their dad into a head spin of events that looked like rage, denial, and depression. He was not just dealing with the imperfect child, but the loss of his mother the day after Easter in 1980.

Mama said if you make your bed hard, you gotta live in it. That was a hard pill to swallow, because I didn't get a proper education in marital life as a young person. I didn't know about having babies or any grown-up things. I was totally naive. Since I got whippings from mama just about every week about something, when this charged up man started his threats with guns and hurting our sons physically and emotionally, I thought this was what it was supposed to be. Now, I never saw that in my upbringing, but my parents were old, and they might have done all the sinner things already. Their initial job was to train the child, beat the child, and break the child. Assuredly, church didn't teach me any better about life, love, parenthood, money, bills, etc. Nope, just bring your burdens and your money to the LORD and leave them there!

One October night, in 1985, the man I married said to me while cleaning his nickel-wood Smith and Wesson Magnum 357 revolver, "I could kill you right now. No one would care, and no one would know. Nobody wants you with all these children, with your seizure sickness. Shoot, I barely want you my damn self!" I made up in my mind that Halloween night that if I woke up the next morning and I wasn't in Heaven, I was going to take my children and I was leaving this man! When he went to work, I woke the children, got some clothes together, and left. I was never going to return. Unfortunately, I didn't use the best smarts that day when I went back to grab some more stuff, he showed up and he caught me there. But, GOD gave me the smarts to get out without getting seriously or fatally injured.

He asked me, "Where do you think you're going?" I said, "There is a lady in my church who is really going through and I wanted to be a blessing to her." He didn't know that I was really talking about myself. I had some blankets, lamps, and some food in my hand. "I know GOD would be pleased with me to help out a sister in the time of need," I told him. Not sure of what he was going to do or say, but he went for it, and I got in Old Beulah, my dad's 1975 Blue Park Avenue, and drove off. My children were with a close friend from the country and they were safe.

It wasn't until I divorced my former husband that I found out about help for the abused. I thought the church was it. I thought all we had to do was fast, pray, go to church, pay tithes and offerings, live right, and God would make a way. Many people died with that very hope. I could've been one of those killed loving on Jesus and waiting for Him to rescue the perishing, care for the dying. I didn't know there were actual places parents and children could go away from danger to safety. You see, when my friend, born the same date as mine, gave me her story of abuse in her own home, and told me of her sister's death due to a gunshot, I had the nerve to feel sorry for her and her story. I thought to myself, *"Poor, Poor C.J."* But what she was doing was shedding light on my condition so I could get out of my situation and have a better outcome. But I was so spiritual, so naïve, so ignorant, I didn't get it. She had to tell me: LOU, LOOK AT YOURSELF. YOU ARE NOT HAPPY. YOU LIVING IN THIS RAGGEDY HOUSE WITH NO FOOD, NO HEAT, AND NO MONEY. I KNOW YOU THINK THAT BECAUSE YOU HAVE A HUSBAND AND THREE SMALL CHILDREN THAT YOU

ARE HAPPY. YOU AIN'T HAPPY!

That was such a day of awakening. It was a rude awareness. It messed up my rose-colored view of the world; my world. Now I have to face my self-hatred, my upbringing, my abandonment, my sicknesses, my children's sicknesses, my struggling marriage, and yes, there was much to be thankful for…my many blessings!

There I was at 26 years old, and as lost as anyone in a botanical and woodland maze. I had many blessings that kept me alive – my dad, my music, my writings, my cousins, my grandmother, and the indelible love of GOD. However, because of all the pain (*and it appeared that the bad outweighed the good*), I couldn't see the trees for the forest. I am grateful that GOD waited just for me. His plans for my growth, hope, and future are now evident.

There are countless events in our lives where we can get lost, because we lose our focus, ourselves, love, God, and our tenacity. When someone vows to love you, you don't expect hurt would come along with the package. If one or both persons in a relationship is hurt, hopefully love and care can be a true antidote to healing. On the real, no matter how hard you try to avoid being hurt or try to avoid hurting someone you love, it seems inevitable; you will eventually hurt the person you love. We may want to be faithful, loyal, or sincere, but human beings do not have the ability to do this on our own. We are fallible creatures and ruled a lot of time by habits and the "feel good" gene. Sometimes, it is because of our callous and disingenuous heart, we treat people with a high disregard. Our family, friendship, marriage, and children are tied into the heart/emotions.

When people's expectancy gets too high, or part of the relationship is compromised, taking each other for granted or making assumptions can become volatile attributes. However, when respect, communication, and the GOD FACTOR come into play, there is a winning outcome.

Everyone born in this world has a plight, a journey to make, a destiny to pursue. YOU are the only one able to do your journey; write your story. Everyone's story is similar, yet distinctively different. With me, I came in the world as a low weight, premature baby with a mountain of issues, rejection, health challenges, surrogate parents, and social and mental challenges. Yet, I was given a gift to smile, be happy, write, sing, and play songs.

I realize two important lessons in life. My grandmother was the first teacher when she said, "Love! Love child 'til you can't love no mo'. Love 'til love come spilling from your veins and out your ears. BUT...Save some love for yourself!" This is PIVOTAL! God says: love ME first, then love yourself, and then other people.

The second, third, fourth, and fifth lessons came from my dad:

- Don't let nobody talk you out of what you can do or what you can be.
- You might give out, but don't give up. Your foot's on the gas, drive it anywhere you can, and you'll know how fast to go.

- You work the job, don't let the job work you!
- Learn to live with a thing, not in it!

My dad had only a 2nd grade education, but he was lavished with wisdom. Every word from his lips was a lesson; a nugget to live by.

Maturity found its place in my world. I didn't give up on me, and a heck of a lot more people didn't give up on me as well. I have reared my children to the best of my abilities. Some things I did to and with my children are a result of things I was taught through my parents. Initially, before parenthood, I said I would never beat my children. But, my vow waned as I learned the difference between discipline and punishment. Love can be found in both and parents need to be clear on both. There was no manual for Louise James and the James Boys. It was a "learn as you go" lifestyle. I was essentially a zealous and loving child trying to train children into people. However, there were practices and disciplines my mother used with me I never used when raising my children. Did I make mistakes? You doggone skippy I did, but I was given another chance. My children loved me and they hated me. I made great strides and huge mistakes. But, I never shut them out. I let them express themselves, regardless of the hurt I felt. What they were feeling was important enough to learn the lessons that pushed us further in our parent-adult child relationship. With the help of the LORD, now I have a clearer outlook on love, relationships, and life. Every day is a new beginning in the right direction. I believe I am a better grandparent because I learned so much as a parent.

I'm so glad I wasn't aborted or that I didn't abort my own

self. I have daily opportunities to write, sing, be a mama, grandmama, wife, friend, businesswoman, a moral woman, and a woman who is always fertile with ideas, goals, and imagination! I am successful because I have love, family, God, and the nature to go get what is needed for each phase.

Know your worth. Say what God is saying. Don't take no for the final answer, because all you need is one YES!

You can change the direction of your life. I was called unsuccessful all my young life, but I saw something different, so I did something different.

Once you know better, you will do better, and then pay it forward for someone else to do better too.

Learn what abuse is and what it looks like on you, to you, and with you!

Finally, DON'T YOU SETTLE for the worst, you are the best!

# MORE ABOUT THE AUTHOR

Juanita Frazier was born in the oldest city in South Carolina; the rich Geechee culture of Charleston to an unwed mother. She is the fourth of five girl children. Juanita, a baby boomer loves family, God, life, people, children, the arts, entertainment, and music. Juanita, whose name was later amended through adoption to Louise Marie, was educated in S.C. public schools and graduated high school in Florence, SC. Louise serves, at present, in a local assembly in Columbia, SC as music minister, choir director, and is on the pulpit ministry staff. She has served as a musician, minstrel, and music minister for more than 50 years. Louise is also a minister of the Gospel. She is known throughout the United States as a soothing Gospel songster. Louise is well-traveled with her musical career. She has recorded seven musical CD projects. She is married to trumpet extraordinaire, Linton J. Smith, JR., her life partner. With his jazz style and her gospel structure, they make music of an incredible sound called jazzpel. She is a three-time published author, she's an award-winning national recording artist, and founder of a thriving publishing company. Her greatest accomplishment is being called mother. Louise is the mother of three alpha males. They have richly blessed her with daughters in marriage. She affectionately calls them daughters-N-love. She is a grandmother of seven. Louise and Linton have a blended family of 8 children. Altogether, they have 17 grands. She is an advocate for special needs families with the ARC of South Carolina as her youngest son has Down's Syndrome. She continues her legacy through singing, playing piano, writing songs and books, speaking, and being a life coach for many. Her aspiration is to record a song with legendary singers, Babbie Mason and Cece Winans.

# Story Six

## BEAUTY FOR ASHES:
## THE PRINCIPLES OF OVERCOMING GRIEF AND LOSS

*Blessed [gratefully praised and adored] be the God and Father
of our Lord Jesus Christ, the Father of mercies and the God of all comfort, who
comforts and encourages us in every trouble so that we will be able to comfort and
encourage those who are in any kind of trouble, with the comfort with which we
ourselves are comforted by God.*
**(2 Corinthians 1:3-4 AMP)**

Listen to my heartbeat. The rhythmic, steady beating echoes the heartfelt cry of a little girl in search of her biological mother—a journey that would last many years and bring with it glimpses of God's grace in the midst of tragedy.

I can still remember walking into rooms, and hearing women whisper, "Is that Ruth's baby?" "Wow," I wondered, "can't they see that I'm a young lady and never really thought of or saw myself as anyone's baby girl?" After all, my mother, Ruth Cokley Fanning, died of a heart attack when I was 18 months old. The younger children in the family and I scarcely have any memories of her.

Our parents, David and Ruth Fanning, had nine daughters, one of whom died in childhood. So, when our mother passed away at the age of 36, she left behind the legacy of eight beautiful children, a loving husband, and a host of family members and friends.

In the years following our loss, I do not remember having conversations about the real pain of grief. The absence of those conversations impacted me profoundly. For years, I endured pain, which would sit under the surface, affecting other areas of my life, until I had to face it, and let the healing process begin in my mind, emotions, and spirit.

Faith in God had always been the centerpiece of our family's life and value system. However, as I grew and matured, I wrestled with many questions: Why did our mother die? How did this happen?

Our father, as well as other family members, seldom spoke about the tragic event—probably because they wanted to forget it even happened. Then, I remember hearing people say to me, "Don't question God."

Don't question God? My mind was a maze of confusion as I tried to process my thoughts. Surely, this isn't the plan of a loving and caring God! How unfair for a mother to be taken away from her husband and family in particular their children who suffered such a devastating loss in the formative years of their lives. Yes, I had many questions for God! And in my young mind, I just wasn't seeing God in all this loss, grief, and abandonment.

On many occasions during my childhood, I felt abandoned by my mother. I could be in the middle of a room full of people, and still remember drowning in an overwhelming sense of loss. My disappointment wouldn't allow me to grasp the fact that my mother was ill, and that she didn't choose to leave her children and husband.

As an adult, I continued to wrestle with difficult questions: What would I do with my disillusionment? My heartbreak? I soon learned that there were painful realizations that I had to confront. I had to accept the reality that I was never going to know or have a relationship with my biological mother. In addition, I would never understand why this tragedy happened. This didn't make sense on any level, yet it was a reality in which I had to face head on.

As a licensed social worker with an educational background in counseling, I knew the following stages of grief identified by Elizabeth Kübler-Ross: [1]

- Denial

Denial is the refusal to acknowledge and failing to state the obvious. Oftentimes, if you find yourself in this stage of the grieving process, you may find it difficult to deal in the truth or reality of your current state or situation. The '*truth*' can just be too hard to bear and face head on. You may simply not admit that you have lost your loved one; or you have not completely realized the magnitude of your grief. You may even go on living everyday life in disbelief that anything tragically has even happened or that your loved one has died.

- Anger

Anger may evoke intense feelings of emotions due to irritation from circumstances often resulting from ill-treatment, hurt, or harm. If you have displayed anger, I'm sure you have done so through outbursts or aggression. In this stage of anger, you may have demonstrated hostility towards others for no apparent cause or reason. You may be feeling or thinking that you want justice for what has happened to you. Quite possibly, you may also feel mad and/or blame others for your loss. You may express anger by total silence at times, not wanting to be bothered. Have you ever rationalized in your mind and became angry with God or any other person you thought could have prevented the death of your loved one, thing, or idea?

- Bargaining

Bargaining often involves negotiation of some sort. It is an act where you may debate in your mind regarding circumstances. This debate may be in reality with another person or a spiritual being, such as God. In some instances, bargaining occurs when you face devastation regarding the loss of your loved ones. Perhaps, you may find yourself making deals with God as an act of relinquishing yourself of pain. Have you ever bargained with God by promising that you would be willing to do things differently, if He spared the lives of you or your loved ones?

- Depression

Depression is often characterized by mood swings. If you've experienced depression, perhaps, you may have experienced noticeable patterns of chronic sadness. Various symptoms of depression can occur, such as difficulty concentrating and experiencing hopelessness and despair.

Depression can cause you to disengage from your regular activities, experience anxiety, frustration, insomnia, and have thoughts of suicide.

You may need to consider talking with a professional counselor about your feelings and get the support needed.

- Acceptance

Acceptance is when the griever come to terms with what has happened – this is when it becomes reality in the mind. If you are in this stage, you'll realize that you'll no longer be able to talk or see your loved ones. To get to this stage of acceptance, walking out the previous stages of grief had to be evident. You have made a heart and mind decision that this is your reality – this tragedy has indeed happened. Your healing process will begin when you acknowledge the tragic event(s), and make a decision to want to overcome the stages of grief.

Emotions can be displayed during a period of grief and loss in different ways such as:

- Sadness – conveying despair, sorrow, or low spirited
- Rage/Anger – a furious emotional reaction, aggressiveness, and harshness
- Disbelief – the rejection, refusal, or lack of belief
- Anxious/Panic – uneasy hesitance resulting from worry, causing anxiety
- Abandonment – to forsake or leave behind

Some of the practical ways to deal with grief include the

following:

> ➤ Sharing your feelings and thoughts about the loss with others or in a supportive environment
> ➤ Consider professional/clinical counseling services
> ➤ Consider a support group with others who have experienced loss
> ➤ Stress management

An important truth that I wish to convey to those going through difficult times is this: adversity and challenges are vitally important in building the platform that you will use to help others.

My journey has allowed me the privilege of working in the field of adoptions and supporting families in their quest to identify background information about their biological parents and family. When speaking with adoptees during the information-gathering process, I've always felt a kindred spirit with the voice on the other end of the telephone, especially when the adoptee desires to locate their biological mother.

My adversities and challenges were not wasted. It was time to embrace a new perspective—a new reality. This event was an integral and irreversible part of the fabric of our family's life story.

God, in His ultimate wisdom, surrounded us with a team of men and women who were spiritual leaders, older siblings, mentors, paternal grandmothers, aunts, and in-laws. Together, they taught, comforted, supported, and prayed for our family in our times of need.

The Word of God states that the prayer of a righteous man prevails much:

*Therefore, confess your sins to one another [your false steps, your offenses], and pray for one another, that you may be healed and restored. The heartfelt and persistent prayer of a righteous man (believer) can accomplish much [when put into action and made effective by God— it is dynamic and can have tremendous power].* **James 5:16 AMP**

A loving God was indeed in the midst of the tragedy, and He showed Himself strong in every day.

There is a point in every person's life where we choose to change our perspective and to take hold of the word of God for ourselves. It begins with a transformation of my mind. I made a quality decision to think differently, and act differently about what happened.

A defining moment came when I embraced a new perspective, and understood that there is a better way—taking hold of the scriptures and getting revelation about what God has spoken in the Bible. I had to incline my ear to God, and be a prophetic voice declaring His goodness in the midst of adversity, because in all things we are more than conquers.

*And do not be conformed to this world [any longer with its superficial values and customs], but be transformed and progressively changed [as you mature spiritually] by the renewing of your mind [focusing on godly values and ethical attitudes], so that you may prove [for yourselves] what the will of God is, that which is good and acceptable and perfect [in His plan and purpose for you].*
**(Romans 12:2 AMP)**

The legacy of Ruth Cokley Fanning and David Fanning is that God orchestrated a miraculous plan to preserve our family.

His amazing grace allowed our family not only to stand, but also to thrive.

Who would imagine that a young man could raise six young girls, who were still at home, after losing his wife? Although, I was a toddler when I lost my mom, what resonates in my spirit is that God was with us.

We were surrounded by members of the household of faith, and for that we are truly grateful. Our family was able to stand and come out on the other side. God gave us beauty for ashes, and He will meet you where you are today when you cry out to Him.

> *To grant to those who mourn in Zion the following: To give them a turban instead of dust [on their heads, a sign of mourning], The oil of joy instead of mourning, The garment [expressive] of praise instead of a disheartened spirit. So they will be called the trees of righteousness [strong and magnificent, distinguished for integrity, justice, and right standing with God], The planting of the LORD, that He may be glorified.*
> **(Isaiah 61:3 AMP)**

No matter what difficulties you may be facing, your solution is the Word of God. Following are some scriptures on which you can meditate:

> *"I WILL NEVER [under any circumstances] DESERT YOU [nor give you up nor leave you without support, nor will I in any degree leave you helpless], NOR WILL I FORSAKE or LET YOU DOWN or RELAX MY HOLD ON YOU [assuredly not]!"* **(Hebrews 13:5 AMP)**

> *And we know [with great confidence] that God [who is deeply concerned about us] causes all things to work together [as a plan] for good for those who love God,*

*to those who are called according to His plan and purpose.* **(Romans 8:28 AMP)**

*For His anger is but for a moment, His favor is for a lifetime. Weeping may endure for a night, but a shout of joy comes in the morning.*
**(Psalm 30:5 AMP)**

These are the key principles that I held onto during my journey:

- Embrace a higher perspective

Go to God for help, support, and comfort. As we begin to study God's word, He reveals the proper perspective we are to have on our trials, our disappointments, our heartaches, and the deaths of our loved ones.

*I will lift up my eyes to the hills [of Jerusalem]—
From where shall my help come?
My help comes from the LORD,
Who made heaven and earth.
He will not allow your foot to slip;
He who keeps you will not slumber.*
**(Psalm 121:1-3 AMP)**

- Cast down strongholds in our minds

Genuine transformation begins in the mind—it centers around our thoughts.

*The weapons of our warfare are not physical [weapons of flesh and blood]. Our weapons are divinely powerful for the destruction of fortresses. We are destroying sophisticated arguments and every exalted and proud thing that sets itself up against the [true] knowledge of God, and we are taking every thought and purpose captive to the obedience of Christ, being ready to punish every act of disobedience, when your own obedience [as a church] is complete.* **(2 Corinthians**

*10:4-6 AMP)*

- Renew our minds and let go of the old

Consciously make a decision to get revelation, and embrace the spiritual perception about the situation you are facing.

*And do not be conformed to this world [any longer with its superficial values and customs], but be transformed and progressively changed [as you mature spiritually] by the renewing of your mind [focusing on godly values and ethical attitudes], so that you may prove [for yourselves] what the will of God is, that which is good and acceptable and perfect [in His plan and purpose for you].*
**(Romans 12:2 AMP)**

As a daughter of the Most High God, I know that we, as the Body of Christ, are in covenant with the Most High, and must be witnesses of Christ's redeeming power to heal and to make all things new.

We are to manifest the Kingdom of God here in the earthly realm—here and now—to bring healing and wholeness to others. We are used as God's instruments to help set captives free from every form of bondage. Jesus Christ is the solution to death, grief, social injustice, violence, teen pregnancy, educational deficiencies, and economic problems.

Christ, the Anointed One, can bring healing to the broken as we acknowledge Jesus Christ as Lord.

## MORE ABOUT THE AUTHOR

Dr. Yvonne F. Keitt is an entrepreneur, licensed social worker, advocate, speaker, and writer. Yvonne is founder and CEO of Leadership Principles Consulting, a training and consulting company. She has been actively supporting and promoting women/children and human rights issues for a decade by serving on boards, committees, conducting workshops, and working in the faith community. Yvonne has a passion to inspire and see people move into their destiny and reach their full potential. She strongly believes every person has gifts to influence the world around them and become catalyst of change. Her experiences include positions in adoption, mental health, mental retardation, and education. Yvonne presently served on the Advisor Board of a transitional facility for women and children and coordinates Life Skills training and workshops for women. She is actively involved and serves on a Human Rights committee for families. She received her Bachelors of Science from the University of South Carolina, a Master of Education from Lesley University in Cambridge, MA, and a Doctor of Christian Counseling Degree from Cathedral Bible College in Myrtle Beach, SC. She was the former business owner and director of The Biblical Dance Institute. Her hobbies include reading, writing, traveling, and fashion design. She is the wife of Curtis Keitt and the mother of Sterling and Amber. Their family resides in Columbia, SC.

Connect with her at
www.yvonnekeitt.com and yvonnekeitt5@gmail.com

# RESOURCES

National Coalition for the Homeless
www.nationalhomeless.org
1-202-462-4822

National Alliance on Mental Illness
www.nami.org
 1-800-950-6264 Hotline

The National Domestic Violence Hotline
www.thehotline.org
1-800-799-7233 (SAFE)

The National Suicide Prevention Life Line
www.suicidepreventionlifeline.org
1-800-273-8255 (TALK)

*This is not an inclusive listing on programs which may be available to families.*

*Please contact agency directly to determine if their services are appropriate for your family.*

# NOTES

[1]Gregory, C. (2018). The five stages of grief: An examination of the Kübler-Ross Model. Retrieved from https://www.psycom.net/depression.central.grief.html

www.ingramcontent.com/pod-product-compliance
Lightning Source LLC
Chambersburg PA
CBHW042053290426
44110CB00006B/169